Selecting and Using Good Books for Struggling Readers

A Resource for Parents and Caregivers

Nancy S. Williams

A SCARECROWEDUCATION BOOK

The Scarecrow Press, Inc.
Lanham, Maryland, and Oxford
2002

A SCARECROWEDUCATION BOOK

Published in the United States of America
by Scarecrow Press, Inc.
A Member of the Rowman & Littlefield Publishing Group
4720 Boston Way, Lanham, Maryland 20706
www.scarecroweducation.com

P.O. Box 317
Oxford
OX2 9RU, UK

British Library Cataloguing in Publication Information Available

Library of Congress Cataloging-in-Publication Data

Williams, Nancy S.
  Selecting and using good books for struggling readers : a resource for
parents and caregivers / Nancy S. Williams.
    p. cm. — (A ScarecrowEducation book)
  Includes bibliographical references.
  ISBN 0-8108-4383-8 (alk. paper)—ISBN 0-8108-4382-X (pbk. : alk. paper)
    1. Reading—Remedial teaching. 2. Children's books—Bibliography. 3.
  Children—Books and reading. I. Title. II. Scarecrow Education book.
  LB1050.5 .W4894 2002
  372.43—dc21

                                                        2002004044

♾™ The paper used in this publication meets the minimum requirements of
American National Standard for Information Sciences—Permanence of
Paper for Printed Library Materials, ANSI/NISO Z39.48-1992.
Manufactured in the United States of America.

To

My husband for his unfailing support

and

The memory of my parents for
their love of literature

Contents

Figures

Preface

I have worked with children for whom reading was a struggle for over 25 years and have always been impressed by their creativity, strengths, and resilience. Early on I found that struggling readers benefited from books that they wanted to read, ones that related to their lives, as well as explicit skills instruction. Quality children's literature provided these opportunities. Rhyming patterns, sight words, rich vocabulary and readable language structures are abundant in good children's literature. In the complex act of reading one important aspect is to match book with reader (i.e., reading level and interest level). Another essential factor, I believe, is to emphasize and use strengths to develop reading skills. In this book I address these areas.

First I talk about reading, what makes the process difficult for some and easy for others. I discuss the importance of determining interests, strengths, and reading levels. Then I share the names of good authors that write wonderful stories with reading levels that are appropriate for struggling readers. Lastly, I have included over 165 reading selections that represent a variety of genres (e.g., picture books, easy reading and short chapter books, longer works of fiction, nonfiction, poetry) and interests (e.g., animals, fantasy, mystery, humor, adventure, historical fiction, dance, sports). Readers will find fascinating stories with readable text and tips for decoding and comprehension. Parents and caregivers will find suggestions for finding and using good books with their children as well as resources that promote literacy skills.

Acknowledgments

There are many people that have contributed to this project. I would like to thank Lynn Stuertz, of The Book Stall, Winnetka, Illinois, for her expertise in children's literature and children's interests. It was always a pleasure to see her warm smile and hear her many suggestions about good literature with readable text. I am grateful for the support of DePaul University and the University Research Council in providing resources for the indexing of my project. A special thanks to the many dedicated parents, talented and resourceful children, and wonderful graduate students with whom I have worked in DePaul's Reading and Learning Lab. And it is also with much appreciation that I thank Ms. Elizabeth Filippo, whose good suggestions and computer expertise helped to complete this project.

CHAPTER 1

Getting Started

Reading good literature benefits everyone, but good books are especially important for children with reading difficulties. For instance, when children listen to or read descriptive language they are exposed to rich vocabulary and grammar structures and will more readily use them in talking and writing. Reading and discussing good stories with well-developed characters and meaningful themes creates a sense of story and higher level thinking skills such as predicting outcomes and making inferences, areas that are often difficult for struggling readers. Most importantly, children enjoy reading when they are exposed to exciting stories and characters with whom they can identify.

An editorial writer for a major newspaper tells about his son who was falling behind in reading in the second grade. Fortunately, *Star Wars Episode IV* was rereleased and *Star Wars* books were everywhere. When browsing together in a bookstore, his son asked if he could have a copy of the book, and the reading problem was solved. According to the writer, his son knew how to read but had not been given anything in school that he wanted to read (Page, 2001)! For some children, however, it is not this easy. So to begin, it is important to talk about reading problems and to briefly discuss questions that parents and caregivers frequently ask in this regard.

ASKING QUESTIONS

Parents and caretakers often ask similar questions when talking about their children and reading. The most frequent are: (1) Does my child have a reading problem? (2) What can I do about it? and (3) Are there early signs of which I should be aware? These questions and other concerns will be addressed in the following pages. In addition, parents and caretakers often hear unfamiliar terms that pertain to literacy and reading performance. Educational terms that frequently appear in school settings and professional literature will be briefly described and related to the complex act of reading.

Is My Child a Struggling Reader?

When children do not want to read is it because they have difficulty reading or simply would rather do something else? Is reading a struggle, or is it boring because books do not relate to their interests? All children need access to good books that they can successfully read (i.e., books appropriate for their reading level) and enjoy. However, readers need additional support in building literacy skills when they struggle with aspects of reading. Two areas that cause problems are reading decoding (associating the oral equivalent to a printed word) and reading comprehension. How can you tell if either of these problems is present? One way is to listen to your child read and to talk about the book content. Decoding or word recognition problems are evident when children stumble over words, have difficulty reading long words (e.g., may omit middle or ending sounds), or subsitutie a similar looking word for the target word (e.g., *through* for *though, were* for *where*). Reading comprehension problems occur when children do not understand what they read. They may have difficulty remembering more than one or two characters or a series of events; making inferences and connections (reading between the lines) that support the plot or character development; or understanding vocabulary terms, complex sentences, or descriptive language.

What Makes Reading Difficult?

Reading is complex. When children have difficulty reading, various factors may be involved. Some children have difficulty decoding words. They may lack word recognition strategies such as phonics (using letter sounds), context clues (using surrounding words and sentences to predict word meaning) or syllabication (dividing long words into shorter sound units) to decode unfamiliar words. They may have difficulty discriminating similar sounds (e.g., sh, ch) or letter patterns (e.g., through, though; on, no); or associating sounds to corresponding letters, syllables, or words. Some readers may easily decode a word but not understand its meaning. For others, remembering what they read is difficult. Some children are so caught up in simply reading the words that little attention is paid to making sense of the story—making connections between what they know and what the author has written. Physical problems such as poor visual and auditory acuity may interfere with reading and require visual or auditory screening and correction (e.g., eyeglasses or hearing aid). Some children simply take longer to learn how to read. Not all children learn to read at the same time, yet for a few, reading is a struggle at any age.

What Can I Do to Encourage Reading?

Find good books that your child wants to read and can read. For example, if your 5th grader is reading on a 3rd grade level, find books related to their interest that are on a 3rd grade reading level. There are good books that relate to a wide variety of interests and that have readable text for struggling readers. Reading is a personal activity, yet one that we share when we talk about books. Children, like adults, have different likes and dislikes. Some prefer fantasy, adventure, and mystery stories, while others like to read about realistic issues that deal with emotions and feelings. Still others choose nonfiction—science, dance, or sports. A struggling reader in middle school emphasized this point when asked what he would tell his teacher to do differently. The student replied, "Bring me a lot of books, and let me read more things I want to read " (McCray, 2001, 299). Here are some tips to encourage the love and lifelong habit of reading:

- Find books that explore and expand interests. What sport, hobby, or activity is number one on your child's list? What does your child talk about, like to do, or like to read (e.g., mysteries, fantasy, ghost stories)? These are clues that help to identify interests.

- Celebrate and explore strengths! Cognitive psychologist Howard Gardner maintains that we all have different intelligences or ways in which we solve problems. We may excel at drawing, dancing, playing an instrument, a particular sport, or getting along with people. Everyone has special talents. Hook these talents to reading about related topics, and you will have an interested reader!
- Find favorite authors who write books that are on the appropriate reading level. Chapter 2 describes selected authors, and chapter 4 provides book selections according to interest and reading levels.
- Read aloud *to* your child and *with* your child. Select a scheduled time (e.g., before bed, after supper) when all the family reads. Show that reading is valued and enjoyed. Let your child see you reading!
- Talk about what you read. Sharing and discussing books strengthens oral language and reading comprehension.
- Reread books. Reading and rereading easy books develops reading fluency and paves the way to more difficult reading.
- Show videos of good books. Rent book videos from the library or video store, or browse in bookstores to see what is available. There is quite a selection from which to choose! (Chapter 5 provides video book titles.)
- Listen to audiotapes of favorite books. This develops listening comprehension, generates reading interest, and reinforces decoding skills when children follow along in the book. (Chapter 5 lists current audiocassettes of book selections.)
- Visit the library and obtain a library card for you and your child. There are wonderful books to check out at no cost! Ask the librarian for book suggestions. Be sure to visit when an author is speaking and hear about their views on reading and writing.
- Provide a book nook or cozy reading place at home and a bookshelf, basket, or other special container for books (see figure 1.1).

What Not To Do!

Without knowing, we often support practices that hinder reading. Dean Schneider and Robin Smith (*Horn Book Magazine,* 2001) list 13 ways to raise a nonreader. A few activities Not To Do include: never read to your children, do not read the same book repeatedly, make sure that your children read books that are challenging because easy books are a waste of time (including comics), and no reading in bed! In other

My Child Doesn't Like to Read What Can I Do?

✓ Find books that pertain to your child's interests

✓ Find books that are on your child's reading level

✓ Find favorite authors

✓ Read aloud to and with your child

✓ Talk about what you read

Figure 1.1 What Can I Do?

words, read to your children! Let your children reread easy books and comics if they desire, and promote reading in bed! It's relaxing and fun!

Are There Early Warning Signs for Reading Problems?

Children have their own time clock in terms of reading. Research tells us that surrounding young children with print, such as listening to stories, looking at illustrations, playing with letter blocks, singing rhyming songs, and experimenting with writing (e.g., scribbling, drawing, coloring) support literacy skills. For example, some children that are exposed to books, hear stories, scribble, and "pretend" read (mouthing nonsense words as they turn the pages) learn to read before they enter elementary school, and for others with these same experiences, reading comes later—in first and second grade. On the other hand, some children, despite early literacy opportunities, experience oral and written language problems that make reading difficult at any age. A formal reading and learning assessment may be in order. Professionals that see your child on a regular basis (e.g., nursery school teachers, classroom teachers) have good insights into developmental aspects of learning and will address concerns, answer questions, and provide information and resources.

Is It Important What My Child Reads?

The important thing is that your child reads! Reading leads to more reading, and reading improves reading. Series such as Todd Strasser's books *Help! I'm Trapped in My Teacher's Body! (My Gym Teacher's Body; My Sister's Body)*, R. L. Stine's *Goosebumps* and *The Nightmare Room* books (readable scary tales!), Mary Pope Osborne's *The Magic Tree House*, Ann Martin's *The Baby-Sitters Club*, and Gertrude Warner's *The Boxcar Children* are all favorites. Often one enjoyed series book leads to the next, and on and on.

There are many award-winning authors that write easy chapter books, picture books, and short novels that struggling readers enjoy. Recommended authors include Avi, who writes fantasy *(Poppy)*, mystery *(Who Stole the Wizard of Oz?)*, historical fiction *(The Fighting Ground)*, and short stories *(What Do Fish Have to Do with Anything)*. Most books are written on a high 3rd, low 4th grade reading level for 4th through 8th graders. On a lower reading level (1st and 2nd grade), Cynthia Rylant writes delightful books with interesting and humorous characters. Her series include *Poppleton* (a charitable pig!), *Henry and Mudge* (stories about a young boy and his dog), *Mr. Putter and Tabby* (episodes of an elderly, eccentric gentleman and his cat), and *The High-Rise Private Eyes* (mystery plots). Betsy Byars' zany *Golly Sisters* (1st grade level), Jon Scieszka's clever *Time Warp Trio* series about three boys and their time traveling adventures, and Louis Sachar's quirky and humorous *Marvin Redpost* (2nd grade reading level) and *Wayside School* books are all too good to miss! For readers that struggle with word decoding, Dr. Seuss provides fun, meaningful stories with repeated word patterns; clever, rhyming text; whimsical, cartoon-like illustrations; and themes that are appropriate for older readers. *Green Eggs and Ham, The Cat in the Hat, My Many Colored Days,* and *Oh, the Places You'll Go!* are good examples.

How Do I Know If A Book Is Too Difficult?

There are several ways to judge if a book is too difficult for a particular reader. One way is to look for reading levels (the grade level of a book), which are often indicated on the back cover. For example, a reading level (RL) of 4.2 refers to 4th grade 2nd month. This suggests that a child reading on the low 4th grade level will be able to read and understand the book.

Book levels are determined by readability formulas that primarily examine sentence and word length (i.e., the number of syllables in a word). Longer sentences and multisyllabic words are considered more difficult than shorter sentences and words with one or two syllables. Readability formulas are estimates and do not account for factors that often affect comprehension. For example, some authors use short sentences to write about complex ideas. Similarly, one-syllable words are often more difficult than longer ones (e.g., *vague* vs. *beautiful*). In addition, a reader's background knowledge affects reading comprehension. Children may be able to read more difficult books if they are interested in them and already have background on the subject. A 4th grader who struggled with 2nd grade reading material was engrossed with *The Way Things Work* (MaCaulay, 1988), a 373-page picture book containing difficult, technical vocabulary and detailed illustrations about machines. He knew how cars worked! His father was a mechanic, and he eagerly looked at the illustrations and identified words such as transmission and gearbox. Sometimes easy books or books on the appropriate reading level may be boring and children lose interest (comprehension suffers)! The best bet is to select a book or author that your child likes and a grade level that is compatible with your child's independent or instructional reading level. (See the next section regarding reading levels.)

Another way to determine if the book is too difficult is to ask your child to read a few pages. If he or she stumbles over 10 or more words, the book is too difficult. If your child *really* wants to read the book but it seems too difficult, read the book together or read it aloud. Others may want to hear it as well! Listening to and discussing good books develop vocabulary and listening comprehension skills, promote sharing of thoughts and ideas, and nurture a love of reading (see figure 1.2).

HOW DO I KNOW IF A BOOK IS TOO DIFFICULT?

✓ Match the book reading level to your child's reading level. Look on the back of the book for the Reading Level (example: 4.2 means fourth grade, second month)

✓ Ask your child to read a few pages. If he/she stumbled over 10 or more words per page, then the book is too difficult!

✓ Ask your child to read a few pages and tell you what he/she has read. If your child has difficulty, then the book is too difficult!

⇨ REMINDER! READ THE DIFFICULT BOOKS ALOUD FOR ALL OF THE FAMIILY TO ENJOY!

Figure 1.2 Book Difficulty

What Are Reading Levels?

Three reading levels are often cited when we talk about a child's reading level: the independent reading level, the frustration reading level, and the instructional reading level. The independent reading level requires no reading support because the books are easy. Individuals recognize approximately 98 percent of words they encounter and understand 90 percent of what they read. The frustration reading level occurs when books are too difficult to read and understand. At this level, word recognition drops below 90 percent and comprehension falls below 70 percent. The instructional reading level is characterized by individuals who can successfully read and comprehend text when support is provided. Word recognition is roughly 90 to 98 percent (e.g., children recognize 90 or more words in a 100-word passage) and comprehension is 70 percent or higher. Percentages for reading level criteria vary slightly according to source (see figure 1.3).

WHAT ARE READING LEVELS?

Independent Reading Level: Book is easy and requires no reading support. Read easy books to develop reading fluency! (98% word recognition; 90% comprehension)

Instructional Reading Level: Book is just right with some reading assistance. (90%-98% word recognition; 70% comprehension)

Frustration Reading Level: Book is too difficult; word-for-word reading. (Below 90% word recognition; reader does not understand text)

Figure 1.3 Reading Levels

Choose easy books at the independent reading level to develop reading fluency and self-confidence. Rereading easy books paves the way for reading more challenging ones. When children read books on an instructional level, parents, teachers, or peers may need to provide some support (e.g., identify an unfamiliar word, explain a phrase, clarify an idea). Children must have successful experiences when reading. Reading books on a frustration level only contributes to a feeling of failure and a poor sense of self.

UNDERSTANDING TERMS

There are dozens of terms that are used in school situations (e.g., school conferences, reports, staffings) or that appear in reading material that refer to literacy or that describe, identify, or affect reading proficiency. Many are confusing to parents and caregivers. The following terms relate to oral language, literacy, and processing abilities that affect reading performance. Dyslexia is also briefly discussed because it is a term that is often used and misunderstood.

Terms Related to Oral Language

Receptive Language

Receptive language is the ability to understand language. Children demonstrate receptive language when they correctly point to pictures of objects that we ask them to identify (e.g., "point to circle, dog, cat, house" in a picture book) or follow a specific direction or nod in recognition when we say something. Receptive language precedes expressive language. It is always easier to recognize an individual's name than to recall it. I heard one mother say her 23-month-old toddler did not have language skills because she could not express herself in words. However, I observed that the toddler was surrounded by print. In fact, she understood many words (could point to different colors, shapes, and animals in picture books) and indeed did have language skills—a strong receptive language from which to understand her world. This is the basis for building expressive language skills or using words to communicate. Children will not understand words they read (reading vocabulary) if the words are not first part of their receptive oral language vocabulary.

Expressive Language

The ability to verbally express ourselves—recall names, label objects, verbally express what we want to say—is termed *expressive language*. Expressive language problems include word-finding problems (i.e., the inability to provide a precise label for a word). Children talk around a word and describe it without naming it, such as saying "green stuff" for lettuce. Expressive language problems are also evident when individuals have difficulty expressing what they want to say. Thoughts appear jumbled, events are mixed, and vocabulary is vague. What we mean is not what we say. Reading and listening to authors that use descriptive language and rich vocabulary help children understand and use words in new situations.

Terms Related to Reading

Literacy

There are many kinds of literacy. For example, individuals with strengths or mastery in mathematics, music, or technology can be described as literate in these areas. According to *Websters New World Dictionary,* literacy refers to the ability to read and write. The Latin root of literacy is "literalis"—of a letter, of writing. This book mainly addresses literacy pertaining to oral and written language. Listening to and discussing good books affect language development and reading comprehension. Reading and writing support each other. Reading extends vocabulary, supports an awareness of grammar, and presents different writing styles. Writing provides opportunities for children to experiment with letter sounds, spell words, and use words and ideas they have read about or experienced. Literacy educators emphasize a holistic approach that encompasses both oral and written language (i.e., listening, speaking, reading, and writing).

Emergent, Developing, and Independent Readers

These terms describe reading development that is supported by early informal home literacy activities and formal school-based literacy instruction. Emergent (i.e., acquiring print knowledge), developing (developing word recognition and comprehension skills), and independent readers (accomplished readers) describe the developmental process that leads to independent reading.

Whole Language

Whole language refers to a holistic view of reading that incorporates and integrates all language systems (i.e., listening, speaking, reading, writing) to help children construct meaning from text. Children are exposed to authentic text (i.e., children's literature) as they read, discuss, and write about good stories.

Word Recognition

Word recognition is the ability to accurately recognize (decode) words. To become fluent readers, children must automatically and instantaneously recognize words and read with expression (Richek, Caldwell, Jennings, and Lerner, 2002, 162).

Phonics

Phonics refers to the method or strategy of using letter sound correspondences and sound patterns (e.g., et, at, it) to recognize unfamiliar words. Children use phonics when they sound out unfamiliar words. Phonics is one tool that aids in word recognition and that supports spelling.

Phonological Awareness

The awareness that spoken words are made up of individual sounds is called *phonological awareness*. In order for children to successfully use phonics as a decoding strategy, they need to recognize that spoken words are made up of different speech sounds and that these sounds can be moved around (manipulated) to form different words. Often struggling readers need support in developing these skills *before* they can effectively use phonics strategies. For example, some children need repeated opportunities to hear and distinguish rhymes and generate rhyming patterns (e.g., pan, man, fan) before they can recognize phonics patterns (e.g., an) in unfamiliar words containing these sounds (e.g., plant, stand).

Sight Words

Children must automatically recognize sight words to be fluent readers. This term refers to words that appear frequently throughout reading (called *high-frequency words*) and that often pose difficulty because of their abstract function or meaning and similarity in appearance (e.g., though, through; where, were; was, saw).

Context Clues

Context clues help readers predict or recognize an unfamiliar word by looking at words and sentences that surround the word and asking themselves, "What word makes sense in this sentence?" Context clues and phonics are important strategies that help readers recognize unfamiliar words.

Syllabication

Syllabication skills help readers break up longer words into smaller sound units. Syllables contain a vowel sound. For example, the word *children* contains two vowel sounds and two syllables *(child-ren)*. When children use syllabication strategies they have ways to break up long words into short sound patterns that they can then blend together to identify unknown words.

Auditory and Visual Processes and Reading

Auditory Discrimination

Auditory discrimination is the ability to hear differences in sounds and words. This should not be confused with auditory acuity, which is the physical ability to hear sounds. Children with adequate hearing may have difficulty detecting differences in similar sounding words or sounds (e.g., b and p). Providing visual and kinesthetic cues (comparing similar sounding words, noting letter differences, making confusing letters out of clay while saying the corresponding letter sound) often help children associate letters with the appropriate sound.

Auditory Short-Term Memory

Auditory short-term memory is the ability to remember what we hear long enough to process it (connect the information to what we know) and store it in long-term memory for future reference. Auditory memory problems affect reading decoding and consequently reading comprehension when children cannot remember letter sounds that correspond to letters in unfamiliar words. Spelling is affected when children cannot remember letter sounds for words that they wish to use in writing. Following oral directions, making sense of class lectures, or following stories that are read aloud in class require short-term auditory memory skills. To support auditory memory, it is important to present information visually as well as orally, to repeat directions, and to limit auditory input so that children are not overloaded with information.

Visual Discrimination

Visual discrimination is the ability to detect differences in objects and symbols (letters and words). Visual discrimination problems are evident when children confuse similar looking letters (b and d; m and w), numbers (7 and 2), and words (was, saw; no, on). While this is common in young children (kindergarteners and first graders), it becomes a concern if the problem continues to persist. Visual discrimination differs from visual acuity, the physical ability to see objects clearly at close range (near-point vision) and from a distance (far-point vision). Children with adequate vision may have difficulty discriminating differences in similar looking visual patterns (e.g., bad, dad). Emphasizing differences (e.g., color-coding the beginning "d" in dog, tracing the letter and emphasizing direction "down and around") and using context (dog and bog will not make sense in the same sentence) help children sort out these differences.

Visual Short-Term Memory

Visual short-term memeory is the ability to revisualize what we see long enough to process the information, store it, and retrieve it when necessary. Visual short-term memory problems are evident when individuals have difficulty revisualizing letters or numbers or the correct letter or number sequence such as spelling a word or wrting a phone number. Was that phone number 234 or 423? Is it "ie" or "ei" in believe? This difficulty particularly hinders spelling. In some instances, relying on auditory cues to spell words is not sufficient because our English spelling system has many variations (e.g., threw, through). Using a multisensory approach to spell words such as seeing, hearing, tracing, and saying a word often helps frustrated spellers.

Dyslexia

Dyslexia is a language-based learning disability (International Dyslexic Association) and refers to a severe and persistent reading problem. Individuals often excel in other areas yet have extreme difficulty recognizing letters, words, and interpreting information presented in print (Richek, Caldwell, Jennings, and Lerner, 2002, 355). Talented, successful individuals are dyslexic. The Los Angeles Branch of the International Dyslexia Association (IDA) publishes a yearly calendar that celebrates such individuals. The 2002 "Outstanding Dyslexics" includes Edward James Olmos (actor, producer, director), Robert Rauschenberg (contemporary artist), Martha Sturdy (Canadian designer), and James G. Morgan (insurance executive and financier). Morgan remarks, "It's all about having the desire, passion, and focus to make your dreams come true" (Outstanding Dyslexics, 2001, LA Branch of IDA). See IDA's Web site for more information: www.interdys.org.

REFERENCES

International Dyslexia Association. (2002). *Outstanding Dyslexics: A Calendar of Inspirations for Success!* Studio City, CA: Los Angles Branch of the IDA (8-8-506-8866).

McCray, A. D. (2001). Middle school students with reading difficulties. *The Reading Teacher,* 55(3), 298–300.

Page, C. (2001, May 20). One-size fits all approach to education. *Chicago Tribune* (Commentary), Section 1.

Richek, M., Caldwell, J., Jennings, J., and Lerner, J. (2002). *Reading Problems: Assessment and Teaching Strategies* (4th Ed.). NY: Allyn and Bacon.

Schneider, D., and Smith, R. (2001). Unlucky arithmetic: Thirteen ways to raise a nonreader. *The Horn Book Magazine,* March/April, 193.

CHILDREN'S BOOKS

Avi. (1997). *What Do Fish Have to Do with Anything?* Cambridge: Candlewick Press.

_____ (1981). *Who Stole the Wizard of Oz?* NY: Alfred Knopf.

_____ (1996). *Poppy.* NY: Avon Books.

_____ (1984). *The Fighting Ground.* NY: HarperCollins.

Byars, B. *The Golly Sisters* (books). NY: Harper and Row.

MaCaulay, D. (1988). *The Way Things Work.* NY: Houghton Mifflin.

Martin, A. *The Baby-Sitters Club* (series). NY: Scholastic.

Osborne, M. P. *The Magic Tree House* (series). NY: Random House.

Rylant, C. *Henry and Mudge* (series). NY: Aladdin Paperback, Simon & Schuster.

_____. *Mr. Putter and Tabby* (series). NY: Harcourt Brace and Company.

_____. *Poppleton* (series). NY: Sky Blue Press, Scholastic.

_____. (2001). *The High-Rise Private Eyes.* NY: Greenwillow Books, HarperCollins.

Sachar, L. *Marvin Redpost* (books). NY: Random House.

_____. *Wayside School* (books). NY: Avon Books.

Scieszka, J. *The Time Warp Trio* (series). NY: Puffin.

Seuss, Dr. (1960). *Green Eggs and Ham.* NY: Random House.

_____. (1996). *My Many Colored Days.* NY: Alfred A. Knopf.

Strasser, R. (1993). *Help! I'm Trapped in My Teacher's Body.* NY: Scholastic.

Stein, R. L. *Goosebumps* (series). NY: Scholastic.

_____. *The Nightmare Room* (series). NY: Avon Books, an imprint of Harper-Collins.

Warner, G. C. *The Boxcar Children* (series). NY: Albert Witman & Company.

RECOMMENDED READING

Gardner, H. (1983). *Frames of Mind: The Theory of Multiple Intelligences.* NY: Basic Books.

CHAPTER 2

Selecting Good Books

What factors should you consider when selecting books for your struggling reader? What are good books, and how do you find them? Who are good authors? Finding books can be an overwhelming task. How do you find a recommended book in a bookstore or library? Where do you go once you are in the children's section? Do you search for the author, genre, or age level? This section provides some answers to these baffling questions.

CONSIDERATIONS

All children enjoy and benefit from quality children's literature. All children have special interests and want to read and learn more about them. Are there special considerations of which to be aware when selecting books for struggling readers? Here are a few factors to keep in mind:

- books that are not too easy or too difficult;
- familiar words, readable text (short sentences and chapters);
- fast-paced plots and meaningful, rich characters with whom the reader can identify;
- stories with believable real life situations;
- books that aren't too long (under 200 pages).

RECOMMENDED BOOKS

Take advantage of recommendations. Professional literature, Web sites, libraries, and newspapers all provide recommended lists of quality literature for children and young adults. Here are a few good sources:

- Newspapers have a separate column for recommended children's books (e.g., *The New York Times,* Sunday edition).
- The Internet proves recommended lists of children award books and multicultural books. *The Children's Literature Web Guide,* http://www.acs.ucalgary.ca/~dkbrown/, provides updated lists of Newbery and Caldecot Medal books, as well as other award winners. The American Library Association (ALA) lists Quick Picks for Reluctant Young Adult Readers at http://www.ala.org/yalsa/booklists/quickpicks/2000quickpicks.html. John Scieszka, quirky writer of the popular *Time Warp Trio* series provides his own Web page (Guysread.com) that suggests book titles for "Guys."
- The International Reading Association (IRA) has several publications that provide children's books lists. Ask your child's teacher about *The Reading Teacher* "Teacher's Choices" in the November Issue, "Children's Choices" in the October Issue, and *The Journal of Adolescent & Adult Literacy* "Young Adult's Choices."
- For recommended children's literature in English and Spanish see *Lectorum Publications,* 205 Chubb Avenue, Lyndhurst, NJ 07071. Spanish translations of books summarized in chapter 4 are listed in chapter 5's Resources.
- Libraries and bookstores have lists of recommended book titles that are current and classified as to area (e.g., young adult fiction).
- Ask friends, relatives, and neighbors!

AWARD BOOKS

Another good way to discover quality children's literature is to look for award books. Many award authors write books with intriguing stories and rich, meaningful characters yet use familiar vocabulary, short chapters, and readable text. There are numerous awards that distinguish writers and illustrators. A few of the more prominent ones follow and are discussed in chapter 4 as well:

- *The Caldecott Award* is given to the most distinguished picture book for children published in the United States during the preceding year. You'll recognize this book by the large gold medal on the picture book cover. Both author and illustrator (often the same individual) create a unified masterpiece in this award category. Caldecott Award and Honor Books *Casey at the Bat* (Christopher Bing), *Smoky Night* (David Diaz/Eve Buntinng), *Grandfather's Journey* (Allen Say), and *Yo! Yes?* (Chris Raschka).

- *The Newbery Award* is given to authors for their distinguished contribution to children's literature. Newbery Award and Honor Books include *Sarah, Plain and Tall* (Patricia MacLachlan), *A Year Down Yonder* (Richard Peck), *Scorpions* (Walter Dean Myers), and *The True Confessions of Charlotte Doyle* (Avi).

- *The Coretta Scott King Award* is given to African American authors and illustrator that have made outstanding contributions in children's literature. Award winners include the poetry picture book *Everett Anderson's Goodbye* (Lucille Clifton), the realistic fiction books *Slam and Monster* (Honor Book, Walter Dean Myers), and *The Skin I'm In* (Sharon Flake).

- *The Pura Belpé Award* is given to a Latino or Latina writer and illustrator of children's literature whose work affirms and celebrates Latino culture. This is a relatively new award that was established in 1996. Award winners include the realistic fiction novels *An Island Like You: Stories of the Barrio* (Judith Ortiz Cofer) and *Baseball in April and Other Short Stories* (Gary Soto).

- Other awards include the ALA Books for Young Adults, ALA Quick Picks for Reluctant Young Adult Readers, IRA Teacher's Choices, and IRA Children's Choices. These awards are noted in parentheses after book titles in chapter 4.

NOTING FAVORITES: AUTHORS AND ARTISTS WITH MULTIPLE PERSPECTIVES

There are many respected authors that write good stories with meaningful themes, fast-paced plots, and believable rich characters with whom children can identify, yet use familiar vocabulary and shorter sentences that are appropriate for struggling readers. This section cannot begin to do justice to all of these talented writers; but it will mention a few favorites that write contemporary and historical realistic fiction, fantasy stories, mystery and ghost stories, and humorous stories. Also included are picture book authors and artists whose stories and themes are appropriate for older readers and a few marvelous poets whose humorous lines and short verses promote reading fluency. A range of multiple perspectives (e.g., races, cultures, language experiences, learning abilities, gender) are represented in these good stories.

Contemporary Realistic Fiction

- Walter Dean Myers, prominent African American author and poet *(Brown Angels),* writes gritty stories that take place in urban settings *(Slam; Scorpions*—Newbery Honor Book; *Monster*—Coretta Scott King Honor Book, National Book Award Finalist). His realistic stories are rich in family relationships; full of memorable, real characters; and offer riveting events that keep readers glued to each page. His memoir *Bad Boy* (2001) is a fascinating account of his growing up in Harlem, trying to disguise his love for reading and writing in a neighborhood where gangs, sports, and being tough were revered.
- Gary Soto, Mexican American poet and author, writes about the Mexican American experience in his novels and short stories. His readable books describe characters involved in everyday situations to which children can relate. Three stories, *Taking Sides, The Skirt,* and *Baseball in April and Other Short Stories* are included in chapter 4.
- Gary Paulsen writes contemporary realistic fiction that are page-turners. A Newbery award winner is *Hatchet,* a survival story about Brian Robeson who is stranded in the Canadian Wilderness, with follow-up books entitled *The River, Brian's Winter,* and *Brian's Return.*
- Jack Gantos, in the two award-winning books *Joey Pigza Swallowed the Key* (National Book Award) and *Joey Pigza Loses Control* (Newbery Honor Book), tells a heartwarming story—sometimes funny, sometimes sad—about a good kid with learning problems and attention disorders.
- Eve Bunting's novel, *Blackwater,* an ALA 2000 Quick Pick for Reluctant Readers, is about the consequences of not telling the truth. This is a moving story on the 2nd grade level for 5th graders and up.

Historical Fiction

- Gary Paulsen's *Nightjohn* is a gripping story about slavery and the bravery and risk-taking of two slaves, Nightjohn and young Sarney.

Nightjohn secretly teaches the forbidden skill of reading to Sarney, for which both are severly punished. The sequel, *Sarney: A Life Remembered,* follows a grown-up Sarney as she searches for her children after the Civil War.

- Avi's Newbery Honor book, *The True Confessions of Charlotte Doyle,* takes place in 1832 and tells the adventurous story of 15-year-old Charlotte who risks her life to defend justice on board the Seahawk, and in doing so, discovers her own true identity. *The Fighting Ground,* about young Jonathan who secretly leaves his home to fight in the American Revolution, realistically portrays the ambiguities and destruction of war. His short chapter book, *Finding Providence: The Story of Roger Williams,* describes the heroic life of this famous American.
- Patricia MacLachlan's Newbery Medal book, *Sarah, Plain and Tall,* is a short, moving story about a young woman who leaves Maine and her beloved sea to live with a widower and his two children on the prairie.
- Clyde Bulla's easy-to-read and enticing historical fiction stories include *A Lion to Guard Us,* about three courageous children who are shipwrecked on the Bermuda Islands in 1609 and *The Sword in the Tree,* an adventure story that takes place during the time of King Arthur.

Fantasy

- Avi's exciting animal fantasy *Poppy,* a 1996 ALA Notable Book, and his two short stories *What Do Fish Have to Do with Anything?* and *Tom, Babette, & Simon: Three Tales of Transformation,* (each story about 25 pages) have rich, believable characters, descriptive language, and unexpected twists. The author makes the unbelievable sound believable!
- Margaret Peterson Haddix's books have strong female characters and exciting plots. Included in chapter 4 are *Running Out of Time* (1995), a fast-paced science fiction thriller, and *Just Ella* (1999) a Cinderella story that takes place after the ball and that is full of court intrigue, power, fowl play, and romance! (This is a 2000 ALA Quick Pick for Reluctant Readers.)
- Katherine Paterson, Newbery award winner (*Bridge to Terabithia,* 1978; *Jacob Have I Loved,* 1981), writes a short chapter book entitled *The King's Equal* (1992), a fantasy romance about a King's son who must find his equal in marriage in order to inherit his father's crown. This small paperback is only 57 pages!
- Lawrence Yep, Asian American author and Newbery Honor award winner (*Dragon Wing*—1976; *Dragon's Gate*—1994), writes Chinatown

mysteries and a fast-paced, easy-to-read short chapter book entitled *The Imp That Ate My Homework!* (1998). The imp, a mischievous character from Chinese folklore, comes back to settle scores with Jim's "ugly and mean" Grandpop, who looks and acts like Chung Kuei, a famous Chinese warrior of old who chases imps and ghosts away.

- Lemony Snicket writes delightfully little gloomy books about the three Baudelaire orphans who get out of one unfortunate event to plunge into another! His series, *A Series of Unfortunate Events,* includes eight popular books so far. Begin with book one, *The Bad Beginning* (described in chapter 4).

- J. K. Rolling's *Harry Potter* books, about an extraordinary orphan and his wizard friends, are full of plots and fascinating characters. The books are long (over 300 pages), so read them aloud if they are too overwhelming for your child to read alone.

Humor

- Cynthia Rylant, Newbery award winner (*Missing May,* 1993), writes a range of easy-to-read, popular series. *Henry and Mudge* (believable adventures of a boy and his floppy, faithful dog), the lovable *Poppleton* (a big-hearted pig with humorous adventures), and *The Cobble Street Cousins* (family stories about three endearing, nine-year-old cousins) are all included in chapter 4.

- Betsy Byars writes hilarious, easy-to-read chapter books with fun, cartoon-like illustrations by Sue Truesdell about two rough-and-tumble Western gals called the Golly Sisters. Books include *The Golly Sisters, Hurrah for the Golly Sisters,* and *The Golly Sisters Go West.*

- Louis Sachar, winner of the National Book Award for *Holes,* writes easy-to-read chapter books. His *Marvin Redpost* series and *Wayside School* books are offbeat, fantasy-like stories that bridge reality and fantasy in ways that keep the reader laughing and guessing. Chapter 4 includes *Marvin Redpost: A Magic Crystal* and *Marvin Redpost: Alone in his Teacher's House* (all under 100 pages) and *Wayside School Gets a Little Stranger* (168 pages).

- Jon Scieszka's *The Time Warp Trio* books take the reader through time with Sam, Fred, and Joe as they encounter Black Beard the Pirate, Greek Gods, and the Knights of the Kitchen Table! In each fast-paced adventure fantasy, the boys barely escape with their life. Chapter 4 includes summaries of *The Time Warp Trio—It's All Greek to Me, The Time Warp*

Trio—See You Later Gladiator, and *The Time Warp Trio—Summer Reading is Killing Me* (all under 100 pages).

Mystery and Ghost Stories

* Betsy Byars, award-winning author, writes suspenseful mystery stories about the adventures of *Herculeah Jones,* a young detective who with her good friend "Meat" will inspire any female sleuth!
* Mary Pope Osborne writes the *Spider Kane Mysteries,* clever mystery adventures about notorious bugs! She also writes the popular fantasy series *The Magic Tree House* with several companion nonfiction picture books.
* David Adler writes about the adventures of Cam (Jennifer) Jansen who uses her photogenic, camera-like memory to track clues. The *Cam Jansen* series books are easy-to-read adventures for primary and intermediate grades. (See *Cam Jansen and the Catnapping Mystery* in chapter 4.)
* Donald Sobol's *Encyclopedia Brown* series requires the reader to come up with the solution! Each short chapter tells a different mystery, provides lots of clues, but ends without a resolution. The author provides page numbers that help the readers locate the answer, solve the mystery, or check their hypothesis! This series is more difficult than the *Cam Jansen* books but is under 100 pages as well. (See *Encyclopedia Brown and the Case of the Mysterious Handprints* in chapter 4.)
* Marjorie Weinman Sharmat and Craig Sharmat write easy-to-read series stories (high 1st grade reading level) about *Nate the Great,* a young detective who with his dog Sludge follows clues to keep the neighborhood safe. There are short sentences, repeated phrases, and colorful watercolors that provide support and information.
* Alvin Schwartz retells ghastly ghost stories in his short books *In a Dark, Dark Room and Other Scary Stories, Scary Stories to Tell in the Dark* (an I Can Read Book, 1st grade reading level) and *More Scary Stories to Tell in the Dark* (4th grade reading level). The illustrations alone give you the willies—definitely for older readers!
* Eve Bunting weaves a good tale about Henry Coffin, young helper to his detective father, who single-handedly solves a crime about a missing mom and a stolen vase from the Ming Dynasty. *Coffin on a Case* is written in short, choppy sentences, Sam Spade style (1993 Edgar Winner—Mystery Writers of American).
* Richard Peck, Newbery award winner *(A Year Down Yonder),* writes humorous and suspenseful ghost stories that are page-turners in *The Ghost*

Belonged to Me and *Ghosts I Have Been.* Both of these spellbinding stories take place in the past. These ghost stories, good read-alouds, and *A Year Down Yonder* (Humor) are included in chapter 4.

- Avi's *Midnight Magic* (ALA 2000 Quick Pick for Reluctant Readers) and *Something Upstairs* are two ghost stories that you won't want to miss. Like Richard Peck's stories, these haunting tales take place in the past.
- Gertrude Chandler Warner's *The Boxcar Children* continues to captivate readers. With at least 86 boxcar mysteries, Henry, Jessie, Violet, and Benny Alden (ages 14, 12, 10, and 6, respectively), are resourceful and adventurous! These books have low reading levels and interest levels extending through 7th grade.

Picture Books

Good picture storybooks tell a story through exquisite illustrations and well-written text. Nonfiction picture books with quality photographs, paintings, and detailed illustrations open up new worlds to interested readers. Nonfiction picture books are good choices for struggling readers because they are short and relate to interests such as *Dance!* (Elisha Cooper) and *I Dreamed I Was a Ballerina,* taken from the autobiography by the famous Russian ballerina Anna Pavlova and illustrated with artwork by Edgar Degas.

Because picture books are meant to be read aloud, they often contain long words and sentences. Some, however, like Eve Bunting's sensitive stories *The Wall* and *Gleam and Glow,* and Patricia Polacco's moving *Pink and Say* and *Thank You, Mr. Falker,* have familiar vocabulary, readable text, and themes that are meaningful to older struggling readers. The following authors and illustrators write from different perspectives and include themes and life experiences that are meaningful to all ages:

- Patrica Polocco, whose Jewish grandparents emigrated from Russia, writes and illustrates picture books that relate autobiographical experiences. One favorite, *Thank You, Mr. Falker* (1998), describes the author's struggles with reading. "Tricia" did not learn to read until the fifth grade, when Mr. Falker, her elementary teacher, helped her to unlock the mysterious code of letters while recognizing and supporting her enormous talent for art. *Pink and Say* (1994) is a gripping story about the horrors of war and the friendship between Polocco's great, great grandfather (Say) and Pinkus Aylee (Pink), both 14-year-old Union soldiers, one white the other black, fighting in the Civil War.

- Eve Bunting, an immigrant from Northern Ireland, writes easy-to-read picture books with sensitive, poignant themes. *Smoky Night* (1994, Caldecott Award Book) describes how a riot, looting, two cats, and an apartment building fire bring together tenants of different races and cultures. *Fly Away Home* (1991) is a moving story about a homeless boy and his dad who live in an airport. *The Wall* (1990) describes a father and son's search for the grandfather's name on the Vietnam Veterans Memorial. *Gleam and Glow* (2001) is based on a true story about a family fleeing their home in war-torn Bosnia-Herzegovina and two gold fish who bring hope of a new beginning.
- Allen Say writes and illustrates magical biographical books about his family's experience living in two cultures, Japan and America. *Grandfather's Journey* (Caldecott Medal Book, 1993) describes his grandfather's journey as a young man from Japan to California. *Tree of Cranes* (1991) is about the author's first Christmas in Japan, and *Tea with Milk* (1999) eloquently pictures the courtship between his mother and father.
- Jerry Pinkney, an African American artist and winner of four Caldecot Honor Awards, paints rich, realistic watercolors that the artist describes as "convincing rather than realistic . . ." (Carvajal, 3). Picture books included in chapter 4 are Minty, about young Harriet Tubman (written by Alan Schroeder, 1996); and *Sam and the Tigers* (1996), a retelling of *The Little Black Sambo*, written by notable African American writer, Julius Lester.

Poetry

Poems are enjoyable, short, and provide practice that enhances fluency. Some poems contain only a few lines while others are longer. Some are humorous and others suggest more serious themes. A few favorite collections that have rhyming verses include the following:

- Shel Silverstein's *Light in the Attic, Where the Sidewalk Ends,* and *Falling Up* contain humorous, offbeat rhymes accompanied by the poet's masterful pen and ink drawings. Some poems have more thought-provoking messages such as *No Difference* (*Where the Sidewalk Ends,* 81) and *The Little Boy and the Old Man* (*A Light in the Attic,* 95).

- Jack Prelutsky's *A Pizza the Size of the Sun* and *For Laughing Out Loud: Poems to Tickle Your Funnybone* are collections of funny poems, many only a few lines long, that are guaranteed to make the most serious grin!
- Bruce Lansky selects humorous poems by noted poets about school experiences to which we all can relate in *No More Homework! No More Tests! Kids' Favorite Funny School Poems*. Also see the poet's own collection of poems in *If Pigs Could Fly . . . And Other Deep Thoughts*.

FINDING BOOKS

Do you ever feel exhausted, frustrated, and bewildered when you have to wade through masses of children's books to find a special title that is on your list? Where do you find it? Is it under young adults, picture books, mysteries, nonfiction, or intermediate readers? It is easy to feel like Cynthia Rylant's charming pig, Poppleton, who screams "Noooooooo!!!!" (*Poppleton in Spring*, 28) when faced with too many options! Both bookstores and libraries have elements in common, as well as some differences. When you recognize a few common classifications, the search becomes easier.

LIBRARIES

General categories include picture books, nonfiction, and fiction books. Most libraries are fairly standard in using Dewey decimal numbers to categorize nonfiction books. Examples of nonfiction categories include history, geography, biography; fine arts, sports and games; and natural sciences and mathematics. Like bookstores, fiction books are grouped by grade level (juvenile—grades 1–5, junior high/youth—grades 6–8) and alphabetized according to author. You'll find some authors like Avi and Sachar in both juvenile and junior high sections. Picture books and easy readers (easy chapter books) have separate sections as well. You'll also find many titles that you may check out on audio and videocassettes. Listening to and viewing books are good ways to captivate a reader's interest and encourage reading.

Libraries also provide phamplets of recommended books. Listings of popular book titles by genre (e.g., picture books, historical fiction, science fiction/time travel, realistic fiction, nonfiction) and age levels (e.g., five- and six-year-olds, junior high) are available. Be sure to take them!

BOOKSTORES

While bookstores vary, most have similar groupings as those that you will find in libraries. Picture books, intermediate/middle fiction, and young adult books all have separate categories. You'll also find series and easy-to-read chapter books in early readers/beginning readers or beginning chapter books (e.g., *Magic Tree House; The Zack Files, A to Z Mysteries*). Like libraries, if you don't find a particular author in middle fiction, try young adult fiction. While books are categorized by age (e.g., 8–12, 12+), some authors appear in both age groups. Nonfiction books are grouped according to topic (e.g., science, art, sports, poetry). Like fiction groupings (and unlike the library), books are listed alphabetically, by author. Be sure to ask if you cannot find a book. If unable to locate your book, the sales clerk will find information about your request on a nearby computer.

REFERENCES

Carvajal, D. (2001, August 21). An authentic vision for today's storybooks: Illustrating familiar tales for a new generation. *New York Times,* Living Arts Section.

CHILDREN'S BOOKS

Avi. (1997). *Finding Providence: The Story of Roger Williams.* NY: Harper-Collins.
_____. (1996). *Poppy.* NY: Avon Books.
_____. (1997). *Something Upstairs.* NY: Avon Books.
_____. (1990). *The True Confessions of Charlotte Doyle.* NY: Avon Camelot Books.
_____. (1997). *What Do Fish Have to Do with Anything?* Cambridge, MA: Candlewick Press.

Bing (2000). *Casey at the Bat: A Ballad of the Republic Sung in the Year 1888.* NY: Handprint Books.

Byars, B. *The Golly Sisters* (books). NY: Harper & Row.

_____. *The Herculeah Jones Mysteries* (series). NY: Puffin Books, Penguin.

Bulla, C. (1981). *A Lion to Guard Us.* NY: HarperTrophy.

_____. (1956). *The Sword in the Tree.* NY: HarperTrophy.

Bunting, E. (1992). *Coffin on a Case.* NY: HarperTrophy.

_____. (2001). *Gleam and Glow.* NY Harcourt Brace & Company.

_____. (1994). *Smoky Night.* NY: Harcourt Brace & Company.

_____. (1990). *The Wall.* NY: Houghton Mifflin.

Clifton, L. (1983). *Everett Anderson's Goodbye.* NY: Henry Holt and Company.

Cofer, J. (1995). *An Island Like You: Stories of the Barrio.* NY: Penguin Group.

Cooper, E. (2001). *Dance!* NY: Greenwillow Books, HarperCollins.

Flake, S. (1998). *The Skin I'm In.* NY: Jump at the Sun, Hyperion Paperbacks for Children.

Gantos, J. (1998). *Joey Pigza Swallowed the Key.* NY: HarperTrophy.

_____. (2000). *Joey Pigza Loses Control* (2000). NY: HarperTrophy.

Haddix, M. P. (1999). *Just Ella.* NY: Simon & Schuster.

_____. (1995). *Running Out of Time.* Aladdin Paperbacks, Simon & Schuster.

Lanksy, B. (1997). *No More Homework! No More Tests! Kids' Favorite School Poems.* NY: Meadowbrook Press.

_____. (2000). *If Pigs Could Fly . . . And Other Deep Thoughts.* NY: Meadowbrook Press.

MacLachlan, P. (1985). *Sarah, Plain and Tall.* NY: Harper Trophy, HarperCollins.

Myers, W. D. (1993). *Brown Angels.* NY: HarperCollins.

_____. (1999). *Monster.* NY: HarperCollins.

_____. (1988). *Scorpions.* NY: Harper Trophy, HarperCollins.

_____. (1996). *Slam.* NY: Scholastic Press.

Osborne, M. P. *Spider Kane Mysteries* (series). NY: Random House.

Patterson, K. (1992). *The King's Equal.* NY: Harper Trophy, HarperCollins.

Paulsen, G. (1997). *Hatchet.* NY: Puffin Books.

_____. (1993). *Nightjohn.* NY: Bantam Doubleday Dell.

_____. (1997). *Sarney.* NY: Bantam Doubleday Dell.

_____. (1995). *The Rifle.* NY: Bantam Doubleday Dell.

Pavlova, A. (2001). *I Dreamed I Was a Ballerina.* NY: Metropolitan Museum of Art, Atheneum Books for Young Readers.

Peck, R. (2000). *A Year Down Yonder.* NY: Dial Books for Young Readers, Penguin Putnam.

Pickney, J. (1996). *Minty: A Story of Young Harriet Tubman.* NY: Dial Books for Young Readers, Penguin.

_____. (1996). *Sam and the Tigers.* NY: Dial Books for Young Readers, Penguin.

Polacco, P. (1992). *Chicken Sunday.* NY: Putnam & Grosset Group.

_____. (1994). *Pink and Say.* NY: Putnam & Grosset Group.

_____. (1998). *Thank You, Mr. Falker.* NY: Putnam & Grosset Group.

Prelutsky, J. (1996). *A Pizza the Size of the Sun.* NY: Greenwillow Books.

_____. (1991). *For Laughing Out Loud: Poems to Tickle Your Funnybone.* NY: Alfred A. Knopf.

Raschka, C. (1993). *Yo! Yes?* NY: Orchard Books.

Rylant, C. *Henry and Mudge* (series). NY: Aladdin Paperbacks, Simon & Schuster.

_____. *Mr. Putter and Tabby* (series). NY: Sky Blue Press, Scholastic.

_____. *Poppleton* (series). NY: Sky Blue Press, Scholastic.

_____. *The Cobble Street Cousins* (series). NY: Aladdin Paperbacks.

Sachar, L. (1998). *Holes.* Frances Foster Books.

_____. *Marvin Redpost* (series). NY: Random House.

_____. (1995). *Wayside School Gets a Little Stranger.* NY: Avon Camelot.

Say, A. (1993). *Grandfather's Journey.* NY: Houghton Mifflin.

_____. (1999). *Tea and Milk.* NY: Houghton Mifflin.

_____. (1991). *Tree of Cranes.* NY: Houghton Mifflin.

Schwartz, A. (1984). *In a Dark, Dark, Room and Other Scary Stories to Tell in the Dark.* (An I Can Read Book). NY: HarperCollins.

_____. (1984). *More Scary Stories to Tell in the Dark.* NY: Scholastic Press.

Scieszka, J. *The Time Warp Trio* (series). NY: Puffin Books, Penguin Group.

Sharmat, M. W., and Sharmat, C. *Nate the Great* (series). NY: Delacore Press.

Silverstein, S. (1981). *A Light in the Attic.* NY: Harper and Row.

_____. (1996). *Falling Up.* NY: Harper and Row.

_____. (1974). *Where the Sidewalk Ends.* NY: Harper and Row.

Sobol, D. *Encyclopedia Brown* (series). NY: Bantam Books.

Soto, G. (1990). *Baseball in April and Other Short Stories.* NY: Harcourt.

_____. (1991). *Taking Sides.* NY: Harcourt Brace & Company.

_____. (1992). *The Skirt.* NY: Bantam Doubleday Dell.

Warner, G. *The Boxcar Children* (series). NY: Albert Whitman and Company.

Yep, L. (1998). *The Imp That Ate My Homework.* NY: Harper Trophy, HarperCollins.

CHAPTER 3

Using Good Books to Promote Literacy

What do you do when your child comes across a word that is difficult to read? How do you promote reading fluency? How do you help your child gain a deeper understanding of a story? Often readers have difficulty reading (decoding) words and understanding or remembering certain aspects of the story. Children may read haltingly, word by word, or race through a section, skipping small words that affect story meaning. This section suggests ways that parents and caregivers can support literacy skills as well as engage struggling readers in creative responses to good books.

RECOGNIZING WORDS

Word recognition (decoding) problems are roadblocks to fluent reading and reading comprehension. Reading is constructing meaning from print, and decoding problems disrupt this process. What do you do when your child cannot read a word that affects the meaning of a passage and comes to you for help? Making use of context clues (surrounding words and passages), phonics (letter sounds), syllabication (sound units), and structural analysis (locating root words, suffixes and prefixes, base words in compound words) are word recognition strategies that help readers in this meaning-making process (see figure 3.1).

Suggestions for Readers

* Use context clues and phonics (e.g., beginning letter sounds). Look at the unknown word. What sound does it begin with? Read a few sentences be-

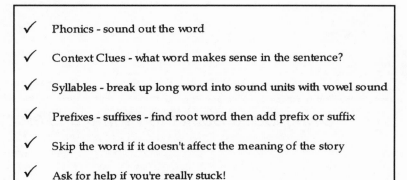

Figure 3.1 Decoding Strategies

fore and after the unfamiliar word and the sentence in which the word is located. What word makes sense in the sentence that starts with the beginning sound of the unknown word?

- Separate the root word from the prefix or suffix (e.g., going). Read the familiar word (go), and then add the suffix or prefix (e.g., *going* = go+ ing; *watching* = watch +ing; *unbelievable* = believe + un + able).
- See if you can recognize a familiar letter pattern (e.g., in) in the unknown word (fin). Say the pattern (in) and then add the beginning sound (f). Blend the beginning sound and sound pattern together (f-in = fin).
- Separate a word into syllables (a syllable has a vowel sound). Say each syllable, then blend the parts together (e.g., rab-bit; let-ter). Say the word. See if it makes sense in the sentence.
- When you see two familiar words that make up a long word (baseball, everybody), separate and read each word and then put the two words together. (This is called a compound word.)
- If you are still stumped, ask for help.
- Keep a journal of new words. Have a small notebook handy so that you can write the new word and a short definition that has meaning for you. Note the book page where it is used so that you can read it again.
- Write the word on a card or post-it and stick it somewhere that is visible (e.g., refrigerator). Use it when you talk to friends. Surprise them!
- Use the word when you write letters or school assignments. Use the word again and again!

DEVELOPING FLUENCY

Fluency is the ability to read smoothly with meaning and expression. Some children read word by word—so focused on decoding words that what they read has little meaning. Other children race ahead, their minds working faster than their eyes, leaving out small words that affect comprehension. One parent commented that her 10-year-old liked to read but skipped little words because her mind raced ahead of the text. It was the little words, however, that lowered reading accuracy and affected writing on school assignments.

Children develop fluency when they read and reread easy books. Word recognition becomes automatic. Encourage your children to read books that are on their independent level. By reading and rereading easy books, readers gain confidence and will soon be ready for more difficult ones. Rhyming, short poems promote reading fluency because of the rhyming patterns that enable children to more easily predict unfamiliar words. Two good poetry selections include Shel Silverstein's *Where the Sidewalk Ends* and Bruce Lansky's humorous *No More Homework! No More Tests! Kids' Favorite Funny School Poems*. Read these poems before bed for a fun and relaxing way to end the day.

Read to and with your child on a regular basis. The more we do something the better we get. Reading is no different. It takes practice—reading and rereading and listening to fluent readers model smooth phrasing and meaningful expression. Finding time to listen to and read with children is not easy. One busy parent lamented that the only time she could find to read to her son in the midst of homework, music practice, and sport events was before bed. But it worked for them! Listening to and reading with his mother provided the 5th grader with the opportunity to listen to a fluent reader and enjoy a good story, to read slower with expression (like his mother), and to be together.

Suggestions for Parents and Caregivers

* Read to and with your child on a regular basis. Carmelita Williams (IRA) recommends reading 15 minutes a day and shares what she heard from a parent group years ago: "You don't have to read every day, just on the days you eat" (*Reading Today*, 8).

- Select books that are short and predictable or that contain repetition and rhyme. Read poetry.
- Take turns reading. Read a paragraph or page, and then ask your child to read. You may want to read several pages or a complete chapter. Take the lead from your child, do what he or she feels comfortable with or prefers.
- Be a model—read with expression. For example, change your voice according to the mood of the story (scary, suspenseful) and when characters express feelings (angry, sad, happy). Your child will follow your example.
- Reread books. Rereading is a good way for your child to practice hearing, seeing, and reading difficult words and to gain a better understanding of the story.
- Make reading a family time when everyone reads a favorite book, magazine, or paper. Share interesting passages out loud. Turn off the television to make time for a good book!

STRENGTHENING LISTENING COMPREHENSION

Listening comprehension is the ability to understand information that we hear. It is the ability to follow and sequence story events, understand words, see images in our mind's eye, and interpret a character's behavior. This important skill requires attention and an understanding of words, sentences, and longer passages. Listening comprehension is required in all aspects of our daily life. Parents and caregivers help children develop this important skill when they read stories aloud and talk about them.

Read aloud favorite books, ones that may be too difficult for your child to read alone but still attract them. For example, the *Harry Potter* books have fast-paced plots and colorful characters but a higher reading level (about 4th grade) and are long (over 300 pages). Limony Snicket and his delightfully dark fantasy series *A Series of Unfortunate Events* are very popular. These are small books with fewer pages (about 160) and a reading level that is low 6th grade, but 3rd graders and up love listening to the ingenious plots surrounding the three Baudelaire orphans. Fascinating, beautifully rendered picture books with higher reading levels include *Leonardo's Horse* (Jean Fritz, 2001) and *The Dinosaurs of Waterhouse Hawkins* (Barbara Kerley, 2001). The first describes Leonardo da Vinci's unfulfilled dream to create a 24-foot high bronze horse for the duke of Milan in 1493. His clay model (of the same size) was destroyed by French invaders, but the huge bronze horse became a reality 500 years later through the work of American art lover Charlie Dent and New York sculptor Nina Akamu. The second picture book is about Waterhouse Hawkins, the mid-19th century English painter and sculptor, who created the first life-sized models of dinosaurs, first for Queen Victoria and later for the Smithsonian Institute in New York City. Both picture books describe the laborious artistic process of creating models from drawings, to clay, and finally to medal.

Read poetry. There are magnificent poetry collections such as *A Light in the Attic* (Shel Silverstein); *A Pizza the Size of the Sun* (Jack Prelutsky); *The Basket Counts* (Arnold Adoff); and Caldecott Honor Book, *Casey at the Bat* (Christopher Bing). Dr. Seuss' *Oh, the Places You'll Go!* inspires and entertains with rhyming verse and fantasy, cartoon illustrations. See *The Read Aloud Handbook* (Jim Trelease) for further suggestions.

Suggestions for Parents and Caregivers

- Stop after a few pages or at the end of the chapter and ask questions, and discuss characters and story events that will help your child make sense of the story. Relate the story to your child's experiences. Ask your child about the story. Does he like it? What will happen in the next chapter? Why does he think so?
- Ask your child to close her eyes and image characters. Describe what they look like. You do the same and compare images.
- Encourage your child to ask *you* questions. Was there something in the story that surprised or bothered her? Are there questions about the characters or events? Good readers ask questions as they construct meaning from the text.
- When you begin a new chapter, ask your child to tell you what has happened so far (i.e., summarize the prior chapter). If need be, look back in the book to refresh memories.
- When you finish reading a chapter, share predictions about what will happen next.
- When you finish reading the book, talk about it! Ask your child to critique it! Did he like it? Does your child want to read another book by the same author?

- Encourage an artistic response. Ask your child to draw a favorite part, an unusual character, or a different book cover. Display the drawing on the refrigerator or some other place of prominence!

IMPROVING READING COMPREHENSION

Reading comprehension is the ability to construct meaning from text – to understand what we read. Supporting reading comprehension is much like listening comprehension. However, with reading comprehension, your child is the active reader, not the active listener. Reading comprehension develops as we make meaningful links with what we know (our own experiences) and what we read.

To foster reading comprehension, it is important to select a book that your child likes, has some background in, or can relate to in some way. Reading about hobbies, interests, favorite authors that write ghost stories, mysteries, romance, or nonfiction motivates readers and develops literacy skills. Reading new words and descriptive language, making connections (reading between the lines), thinking about what we read, discussing, writing, and illustrating meaningful passages all enhance reading comprehension. Reading comprehension suffers when children do not have opportunities to question, discuss, and relate new words to what they read and have experienced, or to talk about the rich language and connections that authors make to tell their stories.

Understanding and Expanding Vocabulary

Reading new words, predicting word meaning, using words in conversation, and writing all help develop reading vocabulary and promote reading comprehension. The more words children read and understand the larger their speaking vocabulary is likely to be.

Suggestions for Readers

- Use context to predict the meaning of unfamiliar words. Read the sentences before and after the word. What word makes sense in the story?
- If the word has a prefix or suffix, first look at the familiar word (root word). What does the word mean? Then add the prefix or suffix. For example, if the word is *unhappy,* separate *happy* from the prefix *(un)*. What

does *happy* mean? Then add the prefix *un*. How does the prefix change the meaning of the word? Read the rest of the sentence for additional clues.

• Think of words that mean the same as the new word (synonyms). What does the word not mean (antonyms)? How does the word relate to your own personal experiences? How is the word used in the sentence? How can you use the word?

• Write the word. Write it in your journal, on an index card, or post-it to put on the refrigerator. Use the word in writing (e.g., letters, school assignments).

• Think of ways to use the word when you talk to friends or family. Use the word as often as you can!

Understanding Descriptive Language

Authors use rich descriptive language to make comparisons that give meaning to their stories. Similes and metaphors give depth to characters and evoke visual imagery. For example, in *The Barn* Avi describes Ben's sister, Nettie, in this way: "She was tall and thin with hair black as night and a sweet face that never could hide thoughts (4–5)." In Virginia Hamilton's powerful story, *Bluish,* she writes, "This girl is like moonlight. So pale you see the blue veins all over" (8). Discussing descriptive language helps readers visualize characters and understand the mood the author wishes to convey. Reading Hamilton's comparison (girl to moonlight), readers have a clearer glimpse of the frailty of her young character. An author's use of words is what distinguishes quality writing and provides endless opportunities for discussing and imaging—both activities that promote reading comprehension.

Reading descriptive language also provides meaningful opportunities for drawing, a strength that many struggling readers demonstrate and a creative activity that supports reading comprehension. Avi's and Hamilton's descriptions of Nettie and Natalie, respectively, are more vivid with their comparisons and provide details for children to include in their illustrations.

Suggestions for Readers

• Reread descriptive passages.
• Think about how the author uses particular words and phrases to describe

and compare characters and create vivid images.

- Think about how you would use similar words (adjectives and nouns) to describe characters in your own stories.
- Close your eyes and see the characters in your mind—what do they look like?
- Draw characters and include details from the writer's description.
- Write your own story (a sequel, next chapter) and describe characters and settings using your own descriptive words and phrases.

Promoting Inferential Thinking

Readers need to read between the lines to understand stories. Authors require us to make inferences to understand character development, why events change, and why characters react in certain ways. Making inferences that are validated by prior experiences and story information is one area in which readers often have difficulty. Frequently, struggling readers do not have opportunities to discuss and relate their own experiences to a character's action and events that take place in their reading.

Parents can help by asking questions and discussing events that require children to "think" about what they have read and to make connections with events or experiences in their own lives. For example, in *Bluish* (Virginia Hamilton), Natalie asks Dreenie to come over after school. Dreenie pretends she doesn't hear her, afraid that she might catch her illness. Natalie replies, "Stupid dorkhead" (36). Questions for readers might be: Why did Natalie react this way? What did she mean? How do you think she felt? Have you felt like Dreenie or Natalie?

We make inferences when we predict. Predicting and revising predictions on the basis of new story information help readers stay involved in the story and construct meaning. Predictions cannot be wrong but can always be modified the more we read and learn. A struggling reader was afraid to make predictions in an after school support program because he was afraid that he would be wrong. He was usually wrong in school and wanted to avoid the same devastating experience if he could! Much persuasion and encouragement were needed to assure him that making predictions was what good readers do. Predictions may not come to pass, and predictions can be modified, but predictions are never wrong!

Mysteries are a good genre to sharpen these skills. Authors are always leaving a trail of clues for readers to predict who the culprit is or what the next event is likely to be! *Bunnicula: A Rabbit-Tale of Mystery* (Deborah and James Howe) and series like the *Cam Jansen* series (David Adler), *Encyclopedia Brown,* (Donald Sobol), and the *A to Z Mysteries* all encourage readers to predict outcomes. Like in listening comprehension, it is important to talk about connections that effect events and character actions and to describe and locate evidence in the story that support what we think.

Suggestions for Readers

- Link experiences to current reading.
- Make predictions (what will happen next?).
- Revise predictions (refer back to what has happened in the story).
- Ask yourself questions. Why did a character act a certain way? What would you do?
- If you do not understand an action or event, reread and see if you missed any information.
- Read mysteries and look for clues!

Developing Critical Readers

Struggling readers need opportunities to develop critical thinking skills. This important skill is strengthened when children discuss and compare books and authors. After reading a book aloud, share your feelings about the story and encourage your child to do likewise. Discuss the characters, the plot, and the ending. Were they believable? Did the author write a good story? Did you like his or her style of writing (e.g., 1st person)?

Suggestions for Readers

- What did you like about the story?
- Would you change anything? Why?
- What is it about the story and characters that you like?
- How would you compare this story to others you have read?

- How do you compare this story to the movie version or video? What do you like (or not like) about the book or video?

ENCOURAGING WRITING

Writing supports reading comprehension and spelling. When children write personal responses to stories, create new stories, or elaborate on what might happen next, they are using story information in creative and meaningful ways. Letter–sound associations are strengthened when young children write about meaningful personal experiences. One precocious four-year-old who had just returned home from having his chin stitched up in the pediatrician's office crawled up to the kitchen table with his crayons and tablet and wrote a note to his mother describing his ordeal (see figure 3.2). He used his knowledge of letter sounds (invented spelling) to describe his traumatic accident when Wayne pushed him at school and the subsequent visit to the doctor's office. Letter reversals and misspelled words abound, yet the preschooler successfully communicated his thoughts! This writing and learning opportunity would have been lost if crayons and paper were not available. Like surrounding children with print, it is important to have writing materials that are convenient and accessible (e.g., kitchen, family room).

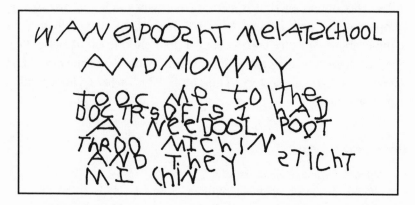

Figure 3.2 Writing Sample

Computers provide opportunities for children to add graphics and experiment with fonts when creating written extensions to stories. A creative bright young student receiving reading and spelling support used different fonts and a human figure graphic to develop a clever want ad for a roommate for Giant John, an unusually messy character in Jerry Spinelli's award-winning novel, *Maniac Magee.* A good story, an interesting character, and the computer created an opportunity for writing (see figure 3.3).

Figure 3.3 Giant Jon

Suggestions for Writers

- Keep a journal while reading. Jot down thoughts and questions that come up during reading, or new vocabulary that is unfamiliar. Don't worry about spelling!

- Write a new story using the same characters. Change the setting, add a new character, or give the theme a twist! Write a new chapter or a sequel to the book. Write what you like about the story, or describe the character that you like the most. Create an advertisement, or write a book review.
- Write a poem. It doesn't have to rhyme. Model it on a poem that you have listened to or have read. (See *Love That Dog* by Sharon Creech in chapter 4.)
- Write a letter to the author about the book that you have read. Many authors have Web pages with addresses just for this purpose. You will probably get a response! (See "Web Sites for Children" in chapter 4 for authors' Web sites.)
- Use the computer. It is easy, fun, and looks professional. Experiment with the font. For example, type bold print for emphasis; or tiny print for a small, tiny voice!
- Get your thoughts down on paper first! Don't worry about spelling! Writers do this. Then they go back and rewrite and edit their work. Listen to authors talk about their writing and you will hear about the number of drafts they write! Spelling is one of the last considerations, although an important one. When you are satisfied with your draft, then look at spelling. Are there words that don't look right? If you use the computer, spell check can help with most words. For those really difficult words, ask someone or refer to a dictionary.

EXTENDING LITERATURE THROUGH ART

Many struggling readers have strengths in art. Illustrating characters, events, and settings encourage and promote this talent while supporting reading comprehension. Have crayons, markers, pencils, and paper available and accessible. Collect materials for collage pictures. Newsprint pads are inexpensive and come in all sizes. Use picture books as models for media (e.g., watercolors, collage, color pencils, markers). After reading a story, encourage your child to illustrate a character, a favorite part, event, or a book cover. For example, draw (paint or color) the horrible mountain troll that J. K. Rowling describes in *Harry Potter and the Sorcerer's Stone:* "Twelve feet tall, its skin was a dull, granite gray, its great lumpy body like a boulder with its small bald head perched on top like a coconut. It had short legs thick as tree trunks with flat, horny feet" (174).

Use soft chalk colors or watercolors and create impressionistic style drawings and paintings. Use the same eight colors as Claude Monet in the picture book, *A Blue Butterfly: A Story About Claude Monet* (Bijou Le Tord). Enjoy the rich, painting reproductions of dancers by Edgar Degas in *I Dreamed I Was a Ballerina* (Anna Pavlova), a beautiful picture book from the Metropolitan Museum of Art.

Use story information to add details to drawings about characters, settings, or events. For example, illustrate a character, describe him or her below the illustration, and write the character's name at the top of the page. To make the drawing more descriptive, use the letters in the name for adjectives that describe the person (i.e., called an acrostic or name poem). See the illustration of Mr. Gorf (Great, nOstrils, fRiendly, Fun), an unusually nice teacher with three nostrils in Louis Sachar's hilarious *Wayside School Gets A Little Stranger* (see figure 3.4).

Figure 3.4 Character Illustration

Make sack puppets. Get a small lunch bag, color the front, cut out construction paper arms and legs and attach to the sack. Use an old sock. Sew buttons on for eyes, or use magic markers for facial features. Yarn makes colorful hair and creates opportunities for styling. Use the puppets to act out a favorite scene!

An old shoe box is perfect for a diorama. Select a favorite scene, draw (or paint) the background, and cut and color story characters out of construction paper. Attach paper tabs to character's feet so that they will stand erect when you paste them in the box. This is a great activity for a rainy day!

Make collage art. Uses materials around the house such as yarn, ribbon, swatches of material, and cottonballs. Draw and cut out shapes and paste them on construction paper or heavy white paper. If you wish, use pen and ink or magic marker to draw shapes. See picture books with collage such as *Smoky Night* (Eve Bunting and David Diaz) and *Wings* (Christopher Myers).

REFERENCES

Trelease, J. (2001). *Read-Aloud Handbook* (5th Ed.) NY: Penguin.
Williams, C. (2001, February/March). *Reading Today.*

CHILDREN'S BOOKS

Adler, D. *Cam Jansen* (series). NY: Puffin Books.
Adoff, A. (2000). *The Basket Counts.* NY: Simon & Schuster Books for Young Readers.
Avi. (1994). *The Barn.* NY: Avon Books.
Bing, C. (2000). *Casey at the Bat.* NY: Handprint Books.
Fritz, J. (2001). *Leonardo's Horse.* NY: Putnam's Sons.
Hamilton, V. (1999). *Bluish.* NY: The Blue Sky Press, Scholastic.
Howe, J., and Howe, D. (1979). *Bunnicula: A Rabbit-Tale of Mystery.* NY: Avon Books.
Kerley, B. (2001). *The Dinossaurs of Waterhouse Hawkins.* NY: Scholastic Press.
Lansky, B. (1997). *No More Homework! No More Tests! Kids' Favorite Funny School Poems.* NY: Meadowbrook Press, a division of Simon & Schuster.

Pavlova, A., illustrated with art by Edgar Degas. (2001). *I Dreamed I Was a Ballerina*. NY: Metropolitan Museum of Art, Atheneum Books for Young Readers.

Prelutsky, J. (1994). *A Pizza the Size of the Sun*. NY: Greenwillow Books.

Rowlings, J. K. *Harry Potter* (books). NY: Arthur A. Levin Books, Scholastic Press.

Roy, R. *A to Z Mysteries*. NY: Random House.

Sachar, L. (1995). *Wayside School Gets a Little Stranger*. NY: Avon Books.

Seuss, Dr. (1990). *Oh, The Places You'll Go!* NY: Random House.

Silverstein, S. (1981). *A Light in the Attic*. NY: Harper & Row.

_____. (1974). *Where the Sidewalk Ends*. NY: Harper & Row.

Snicket, L. (1999). *A Series of Unfortunate Events*. NY: HarperCollins.

Sobol, D. *Encyclopedia Brown* (series). NY: Bantom Books.

RESOURCES

U.S. Department of Education's Office of Educational Research & Improvement. *What Parents Need to Know About Reading & Writing*. The handbook is available for $3.00. Call 888-3661-6233. See the Web site http://www.doe.state.de.us/reading/Parents.htm.

CHAPTER 4

Supporting Interest and Reading Level

This section describes children's literature that supports the following interest categories: adventure/survival, animals, art, biography, dance, family relationships, fantasy, friendship, ghosts, historical fiction, humor, identity/solving problems, immigrants, mystery, nonfiction, poetry/rhyming verse, romance, and sports. While summaries of books appear only once under one category (e.g., Avi's *The Barn*—historical fiction), books may be listed in other categories as well if the story content is relevant (e.g., *The Barn*—family relationships).

These books by no means represent all of the wonderful books that are appropriate for children and young adults who struggle with reading. Rather, books included in this section are recommended books (e.g., ALA's list for Reluctant Readers) and favorites of struggling readers that have familiar vocabulary, easy-to-read text, strong stories, and memorable characters. Most of the novels are between 100 and 200 pages, represent a single point of view, have a fast-paced plot, and characters with whom children can identify. In a few instances books present several points of views and flashbacks, but the strong stories sweep readers along with the different story structure. Many books are written by award-winning authors known for their diversity—from picture books and poetry, to easy reading or easy chapter books, to longer works of fiction.

Each selection includes a short summary and an estimated reading level (RL) and interest level (IL). In cases where the RL is not indicated on the book cover, the Fry Readability Formula, one of several frequently used readability formulas, has been used to determine an estimated RL. These levels are estimates based on a formula that examines the number of long words (syllables) and sentences in a sample of passages (discussed in chapter 1). Other factors such as the reader's background knowledge, interest, and vocabulary affect reading comprehension. All books included in this section have ILs (grades for which the book is appropriate) that surpass the estimated RLs. For example, the intriguing Newbery Honor fantasy *Ella Enchanted* (Gail Carson Levine) will captivate upper primary, intermediate, and junior high readers; yet, the estimated RL is third grade. RLs are not provided for poetry or short text because they are not applicable to this type of scrutiny. The total page count is also noted because longer books may discourage readers. Books are categorized by topics of interest (e.g., adventure/survival), and by genre (e.g., picture books, easy reading/short chapter books, fiction—referring to longer works of fiction, and nonfiction). For a quick purview of book titles by genre and interest, see the appendixes.

LITERATURE SELECTIONS

ADVENTURE/SURVIVAL

PICTURE BOOKS

Title: *Gleam and Glow,* Eve Bunting (2001).
RL 2nd grade; **IL** 1st–6th grade
Summary: See Family Relationships.

Title: *Shooting for the Moon: The Amazing Life and Times of Annie Oakley,* Stephen Krensky (2001). NY: Melanie Kroupa Books, Farrar, Straus and Giroux.
RL 3rd grade; **IL** all ages
Summary: See Biography.

FICTION

Title: *Brian's Return,* Gary Paulsen (1999) (ALA Quick Picks for Reluctant Young Adult Readers). NY: Delacorte Press.

RL low 5th grade; **IL** 4th–9th grade
Summary: This is the latest book about Brian Robeson, the 13-year-old boy who was stranded in the wilderness in Hatchet (Newbery Honor Book). Brian is now in high school and reacts fiercely when a bully taunts him. Upon the recommendations of Caleb, a counselor and friend, Brian returns to the wilderness to discover who he is, what he has become, and what he has left behind. Writing from the wilderness, Brian's short letters to Caleb begin each chapter. (115 pages)

Title: *Brian's Winter,* Gary Paulsen (1996). NY: Delacorte Press.
RL low 5th grade; **IL** 4th–9th grade
Summary: In *Hatchet* (1987), Brian is rescued from the Canadian wilderness before winter sets in. In this 1996 version, Brian is not rescued before winter arrives and must use his survival skills to combat this deadly natural enemy. Brian survives a bear attack with the help of "Betty," a skunk who decides to share his shelter; and learns how to navigate (with the help of handmade snowshoes) the soft, heavy snow of the Canadian wilderness. This is another good adventure story set in the beautiful and dangerous Canadian wilderness. (133 pages)

Title: *Hatchet,* Gary Paulsen (1987) (Newbery Honor Book). NY: Puffin Books.
RL low 5th grade; **IL** 4th–9th grade
Summary: In this first book about the adventures of Brian Robeson, Brian is stranded in the Canadian wilderness after he survives a single engine plane crash. His parents have recently divorced, and Brian is on his way to visit his father for the summer when the pilot has a heart attack. Armed with only a hatchet his mother has given him as a farewell present, Brian must use and expand what little he knows about "camping" in order to survive starvation, animals, rain, heat, and loneliness. This is a fast-paced adventure story that deals with emotional issues as well as survival skills. (195 pages)

Title: *Holes,* Louis Sachar (1998) (National Book Award, Newbery Award, ALA Quick Pick for Reluctant Readers). NY: Frances Foster Books, Farrar, Straus and Giroux.
RL high 3rd grade; **IL** 4th grade and up

Summary: Stanley Yelnats is sent to Camp Green Lake Juvenile Correctional Facility for stealing a pair of tennis shoes that actually fell from an overpass onto his head! The bad luck, being at the wrong place at the wrong time, is blamed on the family curse that originated with his great grandfather, the first Stanley Yelnats. Now Stanley has to dig a hole a day—five feet deep and five feet across—in the hard, sun-baked earth. The legendary outlaw Kate Barlow, Zero (Stanley's good friend at the Camp), and the evil camp Warden who has a mysterious purpose for the digging are only a few of the colorful characters that light up the stage in this exciting, suspenseful, funny, and meaningful story that spans four generations. (233 pages)

Title: *Maniac Magee,* Jerry Spinelli (1990) (Newbery Award). Boston: Little Brown and Company.

RL 4th grade; **IL** 4th–9th grade

Summary: Jeffery Magee is an orphan who runs away from his quarreling aunt and uncle. Jeffery, called "Maniac" because of his masterful stunts and accomplishments, befriends 4th grader Amanda Beale, a fellow reader, and finds a home with her accepting family in the East End. Being the white kid doesn't bother him until someone paints fishbelly on the Beales' house. Knowing that he is different in more ways than race, he runs away to protect a family that he has come to love. Subsequent adventures and relationships follow, but Maniac discovers that he cannot run away forever. (184 pages)

Title: *Midnight Magic,* Avi (1999). NY: Scholastic Press.

RL low 5th grade; **IL** 4th–9th grade

Summary: See Ghosts.

Title: *Running Out of Time,* Margaret Peterson Haddix (1995). NY: Simon and Schuster.

RL 4th grade; **IL** 3rd–8th grade

Summary: See Fantasy.

Title: *Stone Fox,* John Reynolds Gardiner (1980). NY: Harper Trophy, a division of HarperCollins.

RL 3rd grade; **IL** 4th grade and up

Summary: Little Willy must earn money to help his despondent grandfather pay the farm taxes. The small boy decides to enter the National Dogsled Race with his faithful dog Searchlight to win a cash prize for his grandfather. Stone Fox, the unbeatable Shoshone Indian, with his magnificent Samoyeds, is also a contestant. Stone Fox intends to win the race and use the money to buy back land that his people lost when they were moved to a reservation. This moving story of courage, love, and unselfishness is one for all ages. (81 pages)

Title: *The True Confessions of Charlotte Doyle,* Avi (1990) (Newbery Medal, ALA Best Book for Young Adults). NY: Avon Camelot Book.
RL 4th grade; **IL** 3rd–8th grade
Summary: See Historical Fiction.

ANIMALS

PICTURE BOOKS

Title: *Go, Dog. Go!,* P. D. Eastman (1961). NY: Random House.
RL low 1st grade; **IL** K–3rd grade
Summary: See Fantasy.

Title: *Sam and the Tigers,* Julius Lester, illustrated by Jerry Pinkney (1996). NY: Dial Books for Young Readers.
RL high 1st–low 2nd grade; **IL** K–3rd grade
Summary: See Fantasy.

Title: *The Cat in the Hat,* Dr. Seuss (1957). NY: Random House.
RL 1st grade; **IL** K–3rd grade
Summary: See Fantasy.

Title: *The Stray Dog,* Marc Simont (2001). NY: HarperCollins.
RL low 2nd grade; **IL** K–3rd grade
Summary: This touching story is about a stray dog befriended by a family on a picnic. Thinking that he belongs to someone, the family does not take him home. Everyday the family thinks about the dog they

have named "Willy." The following Saturday when the family returns to the picnic grounds they see Willy being chased by a dogcatcher! The children race to his rescue by claiming that he is their dog. Willy at last has a home. This charming story is based on a true story told to the author/illustrator. (27 pages)

EASY READING/SHORT CHAPTER BOOKS

Title: *A Mouse Called Wolf,* Dick King-Smith (1997). NY: Crown Publishers, a division of Random House.
RL 2nd grade; **IL** 2nd–5th grade
Summary: See Fantasy.

Title: *Mouse Soup,* Arnold Lobel (1977). NY: Harper Trophy, a division of HarperCollins.
RL 1st grade; **IL** 1st–3rd grade
Summary: See Fantasy.

Title: *Mouse Tales,* Arnold Lobel (1972). NY: Harper Trophy, a division of HarperCollins.
RL 1st grade; **IL** 1st–3rd grade
Summary: See Fantasy.

Title: *Mr. Putter & Tabby Paint the Porch,* Cynthia Rylant (2000). NY: Harcourt.
RL low 2nd grade; **IL** 1st–3rd grade
Summary: See Humor.

Title: *Owl at Home,* Arnold Lobel (1975). NY: Harper Trophy, HarperCollins Children's Books.
RL middle 1st grade; **IL** 1st–3rd grade
Summary: See Fantasy.

Title: *Poppleton in Fall,* Cynthia Rylant (1999). NY: Scholastic
RL low 1st grade; **IL** 1st–3rd grade
Summary: See Fantasy.

Title: *Poppleton in Spring,* Cynthia Rylant (1999). NY: Scholastic
RL low 1st grade; **IL** 1st–3rd grade
Summary: See Fantasy.

FICTION

Title: *Bunnicula: A Rabbit-Tale of Mystery,* Deborah and James Howe (1979). NY: Avon Books.
RL 3rd grade; **IL** 3rd–7th grade
Summary: See Mystery.

Title: *Bunnicula Strikes Again!,* James Howe (1999). NY: Atheneum Books, an imprint of Simon & Schuster Children's Publishing Division.
RL middle 4th grade; **IL** 3rd–7th grade
Summary: See Mystery.

Title: *Pets,* Avi (1997). In *What Do Fish Have to Do with Anything and Other Stories* (119–148). Cambridge, MA: Candlewick Press.
RL 3rd grade; **IL** 3rd–7th grade
Summary: See Ghosts.

Title: *Poppy,* Avi (1996) (ALA Notable Book, a Booklist Editors' Choice). NY: Avon Books.
RL 4th grade; **IL** 4th–8th grade
Summary: See Fantasy.

Title: *The High-Rise Private Eyes: The Case of the Puzzling Possum,* Cynthia Rylant (2001).
RL 2nd grade; **IL** 1st–4th grade
Summary: See Fantasy.

Title: *The Stone Fox,* John Reynolds Gardiner (1980). Harper Trophy, a division of HarperCollins.
RL 3rd grade; **IL** 4th grade and up
Summary: See Adventure/Survival.

ART

PICTURE BOOKS

Title: *A Blue Butterfly, A Story About Claude Monet,* Bijou Le Tord (1995). NY: Delacorte Press, Bantam Doubleday Dell.

RL not applicable; **IL** 1st–6th grade

Summary: Ten sentences comprise this lovely book that describes the style and color of Claude Monet's paintings in his garden in Giverny, France. Full-page impressionistic style illustrations mirror the eight colors of Monet's palette. A few long color words (vermilion, emerald, apricot, and violet) make this a perfect book for parents to share with young art lovers.

Title: *Diego,* Jeanette Winter (1991). NY: Alfred A. Knopf.

RL low 3rd grade; **IL** 1st–6th grade

Summary: Diego Rivera's life is told in simple text, with only several sentences per page in English and Spanish. Colorful illustrations depict important events that shape the life and work of this famous Mexican painter and muralist. (32 pages)

Title: *Ed Emberley's Big Purple Drawing Book,* Ed Emberly (1981). Boston: Little, Brown, and Company.

RL not applicable; **IL** all ages.

Summary: Ed Emberly teaches us how to draw people (e.g., pirates), animals (e.g., lions, poodles, bears), insects, fish, ships, trucks, and even flying machines using simple shapes. There are few words (some pages have no words) in this fun book that has entertained children for years! (92 pages)

Title: *Franciso Goya,* Mike Venezia (1991). Chicago, IL: Children's Press.

RL 5th grade; **IL** 3rd–6th grade

Summary: Colorful paintings from museums in Chicago, Madrid, New York, and Naples depict the range of Goya's work. The author/illustrator's cartoon illustrations and narrative text describe the life of this extraordinary Spanish artist born in 1746; and his exciting, expressionistic art, which reflected the social and political Spanish culture during his lifetime. (32 pages)

Title: *I Dreamed I Was a Ballerina,* a girlhood story by Anna Pavlova, illustrated with art by Edgar Degas (2001). NY: The Metropolitan Museum of Art, Atheneum Books for Young Readers.
RL 6th grade; **IL** all ages
Summary: See Dance.

Title: *Leonardo's Horse,* Jean Fritz (2001). NY: G.P. Putnam's Sons.
RL 6th grade; **IL** all ages
Summary: Jean Fritz (Newbery Honor winner) tells the fascinating story about Leonardo da Vinci's unfulfilled dream to build a bronze horse for the Duke of Milan in 1452. The famous artist, who wrote backwards (right to left) and was also an inventor, engineer, architect, and astronomer, made a 24 foot-high clay model that was destroyed before it was cast in bronze by the French invading Milan. Leonardo regretted that he never finished his horse, but American art lover Charlie Dent and sculptor Nina Akamu fulfilled his dream. This is a story for art lovers and horse enthusiasts. (43 pages)

Title: *Paul Gauguin,* Mike Venezia (1993). Chicago, IL: Children's Press.
RL 5th grade; **IL** 3rd–6th grade
Summary: Gauguin's paintings (over 20) and Venezia's clever cartoon illustrations depict the adventurous life and art of the French artist Paul Gauguin. Large, easy-to-read text describes Gauguin's style and the enormous effect he had on the field of art. (32 pages)

Title: *The Dinosaurs of Waterhouse Hawkins,* Barbara Kerley (2001). NY: Scholastic Press.
RL 5th grade; **IL** all ages
Summary: Waterhouse Hawkins, English painter and sculptor, created the first life-sized models of dinosaurs in the mid-19th century. Prior to the 1950s, people had only seen fossils and had no idea of how dinosaurs looked. His life-sized creations appeared in London's Crystal Palace and in the Smithsonian Institute in New York City. Double

page colorful paintings splash across the fascinating text. Historical notes from the author and artist follow the story. (40 pages)

BIOGRAPHY

PICTURE BOOKS

Title: *Diego,* Jeanette Winter (1991). NY: Alfred A. Knopf.
RL low 3rd grade; **IL** 1st–6th grade
Summary: See Art.

Title: *Franciso Goya,* Mike Venezia (1991). Chicago, IL: Children's Press.
RL 5th grade; **IL** 3rd–6th grade
Summary: See Art.

Title: *Leonardo's Horse,* Jean Fritz (2001). NY: G.P. Putnam's Sons.
RL 6th grade; **IL** all ages
Summary: See Art.

Title: *Martin's Big Words: The Life of Dr. Martin Luther King, Jr.,* Doreen Rappaport (2001). NY: Hyperion Books.
RL 4th grade; **IL** all ages
Summary: Large print and text by Doreen Rappaport, brilliant collage paintings by Bryan Collier (Coretta Scott King Award winner), and Dr. King's own inspiring words depict the inspirational life of this famous American. This beautiful and striking picture book tells a famous story in an exciting new format that will inspire and inform readers of all ages. (30 pages)

Title: *Paul Gauguin,* Mike Venezia (1993). Chicago, IL: Children's Press.
RL 5th grade; **IL** 3rd–6th grade
Summary: See Art.

Title: *Shooting for the Moon: The Amazing Life and Times of Annie Oakley,* Stephen Krensky (2001). NY: Melanie Kroupa Books, Farrar, Straus and Giroux.

RL 3rd grade; **IL** all ages
Summary: Annie Oakley defeated poverty, abuse, and hardship by using her determination and marksman skill. Impressionistic style paintings and fascinating text describe the remarkable life of this talented young woman who fell in love and married professional sharpshooter Frank Butler, outshooting him on several occasions; stared in Buffalo Bill's Wild West Show; and was a friend of Sioux chief Sitting Bull. The author's notes provide additional information of this impressive American. (29 pages)

Title: *The Dinosaurs of Waterhouse Hawkins,* Barbara Kerley (2001). NY: Scholastic Press.
RL 5th grade; **IL** all ages
Summary: See Art.

EASY READING/SHORT CHAPTER BOOKS

Title: *Free at Last! The Story of Martin Luther King, Jr.,* Angela Bull (2000). NY: Dorling Kindersley Readers.
RL 6th grade; **IL** all ages
Summary: See Nonfiction.

Title: *Roberto Clemente,* James Buckley, Jr. (2001). NY: Dorling Kindersley Readers.
RL 6th grade; **IL** all ages
Summary: See Nonfiction.

DANCE

PICTURE BOOKS

Title: *Dance!,* Elisha Cooper (2001). NY: Greenwillow Books, Harper Collins.
RL 4th grade; **IL** all ages
Summary: Short text and whimsical watercolor illustrations describe the jumps, lifts, leaps, and performances of dancers before the curtain goes up. Details in illustrations inform readers about the energy and teamwork required by a single performance. (29 pages)

Title: *Dance,* Bill T. Jones, Susan Kuklin (1998). NY: Hyperion Books for Children.

RL 1st grade; **IL** all ages

Summary: Susan Kuklin's full-page color photographs of dancer and choreographer Bill T. Jones illustrate the beauty, thought, and art behind dance. Simple one- and two-page text accompanies the graceful photographs.

Title: *I Dreamed I Was a Ballerina,* a girlhood story by Anna Pavlova, illustrated with art by Edgar Degas (2001). NY: Metropolitan Museum of Art, Atheneum Books for Young Children.

RL not applicable; **IL** all ages

Summary: This short story (21 sentences) is taken from the famous Russian dancer's 1922 autobiography. Anna's father had died, and her mother and she were quite poor. This, however, did not prevent Anna's mother from treating Anna to a performance of Sleeping Beauty on Anna's birthday. It was seeing this performance that Anna first dreamed of dancing the part of the Sleeping Beauty. Long sentences make this is a perfect read-aloud for parents to share. The beautiful full-page paintings of dancers by the famous French artist Edgar Degas are exquisite. Notes about Degas and Anna Pavlova follow the story. (30 pages)

Title: *The Dance,* Richard Paul Evans, illustrated by Jonathan Linton (1999). NY: Simon & Schuster Books for Young Readers.

RL 2nd grade; **IL** all ages

Summary: This moving story captures the love for dance and strong relationship between father and daughter as the daughter grows up and the father grows old. Realistic full-page color paintings portray the emotion and beauty of this special story.

EASY READING/SHORT CHAPTER BOOKS

Title: *The Little Ballerina* (Eyewitness Readers), Sally Grindley (1999). NY: DK Publishing Books.

RL 2nd grade; **IL** 2nd–4th grade

Summary: Large print and color photographs tell the story of

Laura's chance to participate in her dance school ballet. Photographs illustrate ballet terms like *plie* (all five positions), *arabesque,* and *grand jete.* Sidebars provide information that ballet enthusiasts will want to know! (32 pages)

Title: *A Day in the Life of a Dancer,* Linda Hayward (2001) (Dorling Kindersley Readers, level 1). NY: Dorling Kindersley.
RL 1st grade; **IL** all ages
Summary: See Nonfiction.

FAMILY RELATIONSHIPS

PICTURE BOOKS

Title: *Flower Garden,* Eve Bunting, illustrated by Kathryn Hewitt (1994) (A Parenting Outstanding Book of the Year). NY: Voyager Books, Harcourt.
RL not applicable; **IL** K–3rd grade
Summary: Simple rhyming text, large print, and a two-line verse on a page tell the warm story about a young girl who, with the help of her father, plants a flower box that will fit beautifully in her family's highrise apartment for her mother's birthday. Beautiful, full-page realistic paintings spread over each page. (29 pages)

Title: *Fly Away Home,* Eve Bunting (1991) (ALA Notable Book).
RL 2nd grade; **IL** 1st–6th grade
Summary: This moving story is told from the perspective of Andrew, a young boy who lives in an airport with his father. His father is a janitor but does not earn enough money for a place to live. One day Andrew spies a bird trapped inside the terminal and sees the bird eventually escape out of an open, sliding door. Like the bird, Andrew knows that he and his father will also fly away home. This gentle picture book reflects love, dignity, and hope. (32 pages)

Title: *Gleam and Glow,* Eve Bunting (2001). NY: Harcourt.
RL 2nd grade; **IL** 1st–6th grade
Summary: A mother and her two children must leave their home to

escape danger in a war-torn country. The father fights in the Liberation Army and intends to meet them across the border. As they prepare to leave, five-year-old Marina is given two beautiful goldfish by a neighbor, also fleeing for his life. Unable to take the fish and fishbowl with them, eight-year-old Viktor gently places the fish in the family pond and empties the fish food in the water. Months later the family returns to their home and garden, destroyed by war, but discover the pond full of beautiful fish that have multiplied and thrived. The author's sensitive, hopeful story is based on a true story about a family in Bosnia-Herzegovina during the Bosnian war. (28 pages)

Title: *Grandfather's Journey,* Allen Say (1993) (Caldecott Award). Boston, MA: Houghton Mifflin.
RL low 4th grade; **IL** 1st–6th grade
Summary: See Immigrants

Title: *Tea with Milk,* Allen Say (1999). Boston: Houghton Mifflin.
RL high 4th grade; **IL** 3rd–6th grade
Summary: See Romance.

Title: *The Wall,* Eve Bunting (1990) (An ALA Notable Book). NY: Clarion Books, Houghton Mifflin Company.
RL high 1st, low 2nd grade; **IL** 1st–6th grade
Summary: This is the moving story of a young boy and his father who visit the Vietnam Veterans Memorial to find the grandfather's name. While searching for Grandpa's name, others pass by—a man in a wheelchair, an older couple hugging each other in grief, and a group of noisy school children. The soft watercolors and memorable text tell a story of sadness, dignity, and honor. (28 pages)

Title: *Tree of Cranes,* Allen Say (1991). Boston: Houghton Mifflin.
RL 3rd grade; **IL** 1st–6th grade
Summary: Realistic watercolors elegantly illustrate the author's first Christmas in Japan. Not wanting to forget her beloved California, his mother decorates a small pine tree with candles and paper cranes. This quiet, gentle story blends two holiday traditions and cultures through the eyes of a small child. (32 pages)

EASY READING/SHORT CHAPTER BOOKS

Title: *In Aunt Lucy's Kitchen—The Cobble Street Cousins,* Cynthia Rylant (1998). NY: Aladdin Paperpacks.

RL middle 2nd grade; **IL** 2nd–5th grade

Summary: Three nine-year-old cousins, Lily, Rosie, and Tess, live one year with their Aunt Lucy on Cobble Street while their parents (who are professional dancers) tour the world with the ballet. To fill the summer months, the three industrious cousins decide to develop a cookie company and sell Cinnamon Crinkles to the neighbors. Their customers include Mrs. Haverstock and her son Michael (a love interest for Aunt Lucy!) and Mrs. White, who is celebrating her 90th birthday. To promote a romance between Michael and their Aunt, the three girls put on a show and invite their new friends. The lovely black-and-white illustrations add to the charm of this short chapter book. (54 pages)

Title: *Marvin's Best Christmas Present Ever,* Katherine Paterson (1997) (An I Can Read Book). NY: Harper Trophy, a division of HarperCollins.

RL 1st grade; **IL** 2nd–4th grade

Summary: Marvin wants to make a Christmas present for his parents. May, his sister, always makes a beautiful gift; and Marvin wants to make one, too. With May's help he makes a large Christmas wreath to hang on their trailer home. When Marvin's parents try to take the wreath down after Christmas, Marvin pleads to leave it up. As the months pass, Marvin does not want to take his wreath down! Finally, in the summer when the wreath has turned brown, Marvin gives permission that his parents may take down his wreath. But it is too late. Marvin's beaming dad lifts Marvin up to see a bird's nest with six tiny eggs nestled in the wreath's branches! (48 pages)

Title: *Summer Party—The Cobble Street Cousins,* by Cynthia Rylant (2001). NY: Simon & Schuster Books for Young Readers, an imprint of Simon & Schuster Children's Publishing Division.

RL middle 2nd grade; **IL** 2nd–5th grade

Summary: Nine-year-old cousins Lily and Rosie (sisters) and Tess have lived with their Aunt Lucy while their parents are away on a world dancing tour. Now Lily and Rosie's parents and Tess' mother are returning and the girls must leave Aunt Lucy, her friend Michael, and each other. To cheer themselves up they plan a summer party where they will invite their parents, Aunt Lucy, and Michael. (Read *In Aunt Lucy's House* to find out how the cousins brought Michael and Aunt Lucy together!) When Michael proposes at the party, the girls are overjoyed because they will return in August to plan and attend a summer wedding! (84 pages)

Title: *The Josefina Story Quilt,* Eleanor Coerr (1986). NY: Harper Trophy, a division of HarperCollins.
RL 2nd grade; **IL** 2nd–4th grade
Summary: See Historical Fiction.

FICTION

Title: *Esperanza Rising,* Pam Muñoz Ryan (2000). New York, NY: Scholastic Press.
RL 5th grade; **IL** 5th–8th grade
Summary: See Identity/Solving Problems.

Title: *Mother and Daughter* (pp. 60–68), from *Baseball in April and Other Stories,* Gary Soto (1990). NY: Harcourt.
RL middle 5th grade; **IL** 3rd–7th grade
Summary: Yollie Moreno wants to go to the 8th grade fall dance but needs a new outfit. Yollie's mother, a large woman who wears muumuus and eats sweets, cannot afford to buy a new dress but thinks of the perfect solution. She will dye Yollie's white summer dress black! Yollie is quite pleased with her new, sophisticated-looking dress until it begins to rain and the dress drips dye! When Yollie is asked to go to a movie, Mrs. Moreno decides to use her savings to buy Yolie a new blouse and skirt that will not bleed in any kind of weather. (9 pages)

Title: *Stone Fox,* John Reynolds Gardiner (1980). NY: Harper Trophy, a division of HarperCollins.
RL 3rd grade; **IL** 4th grade and up

Summary: See Adventure/Survival.

Title: *Superfudge,* Judy Blume (1980). NY: Bantam Doubleday Dell.

RL low 4th grade; **IL** 3rd–7th grade

Summary: See Humor.

Title: *The Barn,* Avi (1994) (An ALA Notable Book). NY: Avon Books.

RL low 5th grade; **IL** 3rd–7th grade

Summary: See Historical Fiction.

Title: *The Skin I'm In,* Sharon G. Flake (1998) (Coretta Scott King AwardALA Quick Picks for Reluctant Young Adult ReadersALA Best Book for Young Adults). NY: Jump at the Sun—Hyperion Paperbacks for Children.

RL middle 3rd grade; **IL** 7th grade and up

Summary: See Identity/Solving Problems.

FANTASY

PICTURE BOOKS

Title: *Go, Dog. Go!,* P. D. Eastman (1961). NY: Random House.

RL low 1st grade; **IL** K–3rd grade

Summary: Big and little dogs; black and white dogs; dogs with hats; dogs going in and out, sitting on and under trees; plus many more action activities help readers learn words and concepts. Cartoon-like illustrations support understanding of spatial concepts in this humorous, easy-to-read picture book. (64 pages)

Title: *Green Eggs and Ham,* Dr. Seuss (1960). NY: Random House.

RL 1st grade; **IL** 1st–4th grade

Summary: The delightful rhyming text describes the numerous ways that Sam-I-Am tries to coax the Knox into liking green eggs and ham. Repetition and rhyme make this an easy-to-read, fun, successful experience. Be sure to look at other Dr. Seuss' books including *The Cat in the Hat* and *Fox in Socks.* (62 pages)

Title: *I Like Me,* Nancy Carlson (1988). NY: Viking Kestrel, Penguin Group.
RL 1st grade; **IL** K–3rd grade
Summary: See Identity/Solving Problems.

Title: *Oh, the Places You'll Go!,* (1990). Dr. Seuss. NY: Random House.
RL 1st grade; **IL** 3rd grade and up
Summary: See Identity/ Solving Problems.

Title: *Sam and the Tigers,* Julius Lester, illustrated by Jerry Pinkney (1996). NY: Dial Books for Young Readers.
RL high 1st, low 2nd grade; **IL** K–3rd grade
Summary: Julius Lester, noted African American writer, retells *Little Black Sambo,* a story he says that he read at age seven and has remembered for 50 years! In this retelling (as Lester puts it, "without the historical baggage but retaining the fun"), all the people are named Sam; and animals and people live together, dressed in elegant attire, except the tigers that Sam outwits. Each tiger he meets he bargains for his life by giving away his clothes—first his elegant red coat, then his purple pants, yellow shirt, fancy shoes and finally, green umbrella. Each proclaiming that they are the finest, the tigers chase each other's tails until all become butter, enough for a glorious pancake supper for Sam, his family, and the neighbors! Jerry Pinkney's bright, colorful, imaginative paintings (trees have faces as well) splash across each page and sparkle with Julius Lester's clever storytelling. This is a fun book to read aloud. (33 pages)

Title: *The Cat in the Hat,* Dr. Seuss (1957). NY: Random House.
RL 1st grade; **IL** K–3rd grade
Summary: The Cat in the Hat and his friends, Thing One and Thing Two, visit two bored children. Rhyming text and cartoon-like illustrations delightfully describe the fun, games, and bedlam that the Cat in the Hat brings to Sally, her brother, their pet fish, and their home! (61 pages and only 223 different words)

EASY READING/SHORT CHAPTER BOOKS

Title: *A Mouse Called Wolf,* Dick King-Smith (1997). NY: Crown Publishers, a division of Random House.

RL 2nd grade; **IL** 2nd–5th grade

Summary: Wolfgang Amadeus Mouse ("Wolf" for short) is the youngest and most talented of his mother's 13 children. Wolf can sing! The mouse hole is close to Mrs. Honeybee's piano and the tiny mouse listens to Mrs. Honeybee play, wishing that he could sing along with her. The two musicians become good friends after Mrs. Honeybee tempts Wolf to come closer with chocolates positioned in strategic places on her piano! One day when Mrs. Honeybee trips and falls, it is Wolf's clear voice that brings the elderly widow help. (98 pages)

Title: *Aunt Eater Loves A Mystery,* Doug Cushman (1987) (An I Can Read Book). NY: Harper Trophy, a division of HarperCollins.

RL low 2nd grade; **IL** 1st–3rd grade

Summary: Four short stories with colorful illustrations describe Aunt Eater's adventures as she creates problems and solves her own mysteries. From a stolen bag and a looming shadow to a mysterious visitor and a lost cat, Aunt Eater's escapades are humorous and predictable! (64 pages)

Title: *Billy the Bird,* Dick King-Smith (2001). NY: Hyperion Books for Children.

RL 3rd grade; **IL** 1st–3rd grade

Summary: Eight-year-old Mary Bird discovers that her four-year-old brother Billy can fly when the moon is full. Lilyleaf (the cat) and Mr. Keylock (the pet guinia) are also in on the secret. After exciting adventures (e.g., Billy frightens the cat robber), the lunar eclipse robs Billy of his flying magic. (67 pages)

Title: *Detective Dinosaur Lost and Found,* James Skofield (1998) (An I Can Read Book). NY: Harper Trophy, a division of Harper-Collins.

RL low 2nd grade; **IL** 1st–3rd grade

Summary: Three short stories tell about the adventures of Detective Dinosaur and Officer Pterodactyl. Lost-and-found cases include Baby Penny Dinosaur, a small kitten who really isn't lost at all, and finally Detective Dinosaur himself! Dinosaur names appear throughout these short, humorous stories; but the author provides pronunciation guidelines that dinosaur fans will easily master. (48 pages)

Title: *Ghost Town at Sundown,* Mary Pope Osborne (1997). NY: Random House.
RL 2nd grade; **IL** 1st–4th grade
Summary: See Mystery.

Title: *In a Dark, Dark Room and Other Scary Stories,* retold by Alvin Schwartz (1984) (An I Can Read Book). NY: HarperCollins.
RL low 1st grade; **IL** 1st–4th grade.
Summary: See Ghosts.

Title: *Jane On Her Own: A Catwings Tale,* Ursula K. Le Guin (1999). NY: Scholastic.
RL low 3rd grade; **IL** 1st–4th grade
Summary: Jane and her brothers and sisters who are catwings (cats with wings), live at Overhill Farm. Jane is bored living at the farm and wants to fly away to the city. Her sister warns her not to leave because being different is dangerous. Wanting adventure, Jane leaves the safety of the farm and flies to the city. Flying into an open window searching for food, Jane meets the friendly "Poppa," who quietly closes and locks the window. He names Jane "Miss Mystery Cat" and puts her on display for fame and money. Jane yearns to be free once more and plans her escape. This is a short story with an important message. (42 pages)

Title: *Marvin Redpost A Magic Crystal?,* Louis Sachar (2000). NY: Random House.
RL middle 2nd grade; **IL** 2nd–5th grade
Summary: See Humor.

Title: *Marvin Redpost Alone in His Teacher's House,* Louis Sachar (1994). NY: Random House.

RL low 2nd grade; **IL** 1st–4th grade
Summary: See Humor.

Title: *Marvin Redpost: Is He A Girl?*, Louis Sachar (1993). NY: Random House.
RL high 1st grade; **IL** 1st–4th grade
Summary: See Humor.

Title: *More Scary Stories to Tell in the Dark*, retold by Alvin Schwartz (1984).
RL 4th grade; **IL** 4th grade and up
Summary: See Ghosts.

Title: *Mouse Soup*, Arnold Lobel (1977) (An I Can Read Book). NY: Harper Trophy, a division of HarperCollins.
RL 1st grade; **IL** 1st–3rd grade
Summary: A mouse finds himself inside a weasel's pot ready to be cooked for soup! The clever mouse tells the weasel that the soup will taste better if it has stories in it. After telling four stories, the mouse instructs the weasel to find bees, mud, stones, and a thorn bush (important objects in each story) to put in the soup. By the time weasel returns, mouse is safely at home reading a good book! (64 pages)

Title: *Mouse Tales*, Arnold Lobel (1972) (An I Can Read Book). NY: Harper Trophy, a division of HarperCollins.
RL 1st grade; **IL** 1st–3rd grade
Summary: Father mouse tells his children seven short tales if they promise to go to sleep when he is done! Humorous stories that include an old mouse who discovers that chewing gum will hold up his pants and a young mouse who bathes until he is clean (and the town is covered with water from an over-full tub!) make up this delightful collection of stories and illustrations by well-known author and artist Arnold Lobel. (64 pages)

Title: *Owl at Home*, Arnold Lobel (1975). NY: Harper Trophy, HarperCollins Children's Books.
RL middle 1st grade; **IL** 1st–3rd grade

Summary: Five delightful chapters tell the adventures of likable Owl and the hazards he encounters at home. Finding bumps under the blanket (his own feet!), discovering Winter knocking at the door, and wanting to locate upstairs and downstairs at the same time, Owl humorously faces the mysteries and adventures that surround him. (64 pages)

Title: *Poppleton in Fall,* Cynthia Rylant (1999). NY: Scholastic.

RL low 1st grade; **IL** 1st–3rd grade

Summary: Three, easy-to-read short chapters (stories) about Poppleton's adventures in the fall. The first story, "The Geese," is about geese flying south over Poppleton's home. Poppleton invites first two, then five, then eight geese inside for cookies. All birds have rhyming names and Poppleton is talking in rhymes before the day is out! In "The Coat," Poppleton thinks that he is too big after Zacko says that he cannot make a fall coat large enough to fit the sensitive pig. Poppleton's friend, Cherry Sue, points out that the tailor, Zaco, is a ferret, far too small to sew for a big, proud pig! The third story, just as delightful as the first two, features Cherry Sue, who changes her "plain" pancake order to blueberry to help Poppleton satisfy the cooks! Mark Teague, noted illustrator, paints this wonderful pig and his friends. This series includes *Poppleton, Poppleton and Friends,* and *Poppleton Everyday.* (48 pages)

Title: *Poppleton in Spring,* Cynthia Rylant (1999). NY: Scholastic.

RL low 1st grade; **IL** 1st–3rd grade

Summary: Three individual stories with short sentences and familiar, repetitive language that describe Poppleton and his friends during his adventures of spring cleaning, selecting a bicycle, and sleeping in a tent (chapters 1, 2, and 3 respectively). All three chapters (i.e., stories) have universal themes. For instance, after spring cleaning Poppleton has accumulated more "things" from his good friend Cherry Sue than he has gotten rid of! While sleeping in a tent, Poppleton has time to read, think, and pay attention. While others are sleeping he witnesses the budding of a spring flower. What things we see when we pay attention! And, while trying to select a bicycle, Poppleton is faced with too many choices and screams, "Noooooooooo!!!!!" (p. 28), an emotion familiar to us all! (48 pages)

Title: *Spider Kane and the Mystery at Jumbo Nightcrawler's,* Mary Pope Osborne (1999). NY: Random House.
RL 4th grade; **IL** 3rd–5th grade
Summary: See Mystery.

Title: *The High-Rise Private Eyes: The Case of the Puzzling Possum,* Cynthia Rylant (2001). Hong Kong, S. China Printing: Greenwillow Books, HarperCollins.
RL 2nd grade; **IL** 1st–4th grade
Summary: A trombone from Mr. Riley's music store disappears, than reappears, then disappears, then reappears. The only clues left in the display window where the trombone rests are muddy prints and a piece of straw. Who is the thief? Bunny Brown and Jack Jones, the practical bunny and sensitive raccoon, try to solve the mystery. The clues lead the detectives on a hayride where they discover the trombone and a possum musician who has a sad story to tell. It is Bunny's clever plan that helps possum finance the trombone while helping Mr. Riley in his music store. The repeated vocabulary and delightful illustrations support the author's clever story. (48 pages)

Title: *The Imp That Ate My Homework!,* Lawrence Yep (1998). NY: Harper Trophy, a division of HarperCollins.
RL 2nd grade; **IL** 3rd–7th grade
Summary: Jim must interview his Grandpop for a homework assignment. Grandpop is native-born Chinese and has the reputation of being the meanest man in Chinatown! One morning Jim finds an Imp in his bedroom, doing all sorts of mean and dangerous things (e.g., eating his homework)! When he runs to tell his mom and dad, the Imp causes destruction, leaving Jim to take the blame. Only Grandpop is a match for the four-armed, green-furred Imp! Is Grandpop the reincarnated Chung Kuei—the famous folklore character who chases imps and ghosts away? Will Grandpop finally agree to be interviewed? This is a clever story about Chinese folklore, values, and family relations. Lawrence Yep is a prominent Asian American writer who has received the Newbery Honor and the International Reading Association Children's Book Award. (87 pages)

Title: *The King's Equal,* Katherine Paterson (1992) (Trophy Chapter Book, International Reading Association [IRA] Teachers' Choices). NY: Harper Trophy, a division of HarperCollins.

RL 3rd grade; **IL** 2nd–5th grade

Summary: A young prince is told by his dying father that he will only inherit the crown when he finds a woman equal in beauty, intelligence, and wealth. The selfish prince learns about true wealth when he meets a mysterious Wolf in the forest and Rosamund, the lovely, kind, and industrious daughter of a farmer. This is an enchanting, short fairy tale written in easy-to-read print. (57 pages)

Title: *The Time Warp Trio: It's All Greek to Me,* Jon Scieszka (1999). NY: Puffin Books.

RL 2nd grade; **IL** 2nd–6th grade

Summary: Sam, Fred, and Joe (the time warp trio) are ready to go on stage in their school play "The Myth of Power," a class project that is a spoof on Greek mythology. All of a sudden they come face-to-face with Cerberus, the three-headed dog of Greek mythology that is REAL! The boys have been transmitted through time to where their class play takes place, Mt. Olympus, because of *The Book,* a magic time-warping book that Joe has in his back-pack. The boys meet up with Gods Zeus, Aphrodite, Apollo, Ares, and Athena; and they must use their heads to get out of life-threatening and hilarious situations. (69 pages)

Title: *The Time Warp Trio: See You Later, Gladiator,* Jon Scieszka (2000). NY: Penguin Group.

RL high 2nd grade; **IL** 2nd–6th grade

Summary: As Joe, Jake, and Fred are jumping and rough-housing on the bed, The Book falls off the bookshelf with a page flipped open to ancient Rome. The three boys are whisked away before they know it and come face-to-face with an angry Brutus, a trident- throwing Gladiator! When the boys meet up with the Professor, a teacher in Carthage that was sold into slavery, the four devise a plan that will rescue all from the dangers in the bloody Colosseum! (85 pages)

Title: *The Time Warp Trio: Summer Reading Is Killing Me!*, Jon Scieszka (1998). NY: Puffin Books.

RL high 2nd grade; **IL** 2nd–6th grade

Summary: When Fred stuffs the summer reading list in a book on the shelf he thinks he is getting rid of work for himself and his two friends! Only the book is not an ordinary book, it is *The Book!* In this adventure the time warp trio is whisked away to Hoboken where all the evil characters in their summer reading list are after heroes and heroines. Charlotte, Frog and Toad, Pippi Longstocking, Mary Poppins, and Winnie-the-Pooh are being dragged, pulled, and carried away by the likes of the Headless Horseman, Dracula, and Frankenstein. The culprit is Teddy Bear, who wants some respect and the lead in all the books! Joe, Fred, and Sam must save the noble story characters and escape the evil hands of Teddy Bear and his henchman, the Devil! (69 pages)

Title: *The Zack Files: The Boy Who Cried Bigfoot*, Dan Greenburg (2000). NY: Grosset & Dunlap, a division of Penguin Putnam books for Young Readers.

RL middle 2nd grade; **IL** 2nd–5th grade

Summary: Ten-year-old Zack lives with his father in New York City. Zack finally talks his dad into letting him go to Summer Camp Weno wanna-getta-wedgee with his best friend Spence. When the boys befriend Freddy, the Bigfoot monster that supposedly haunts the camp, only the boys know that he is a kind monster and one that they must protect from his bad reputation! This is one of the humorous stories in the series about The Zack Files. (58 pages)

FICTION

Title: *A Series of Unfortunate Events: The Bad Beginning*, Lemony Snicket (1999). NY: HarperCollins.

RL 6th grade; **IL** 3rd grade and up

Summary: Violet Baudelaire, age 14, her brother Klaus, age 12, and their baby sister Sunny are suddenly orphaned when their parents die in a fire. The three unfortunate orphans are sent to live with their greedy distant cousin, Count Olaf, who will stop at nothing to get their fortune!

This darkly funny, fast-paced book leaves the children safe from Olaf's clutches, but more unfortunate events are sure to come! This is the first book in the series. (162 pages)

Title: *Bunnicula: A Rabbit-Tale of Mystery,* Deborah and James Howe (1979). NY: Avon Books.
RL 3rd grade; **IL** 3rd–7th grade
Summary: See Humor.

Title: *Bunnicula Strikes Again!,* James Howe (1999). NY: Avon Books.
RL 3rd grade; **IL** 3rd–7th grade
Summary: See Humor.

Title: *Ella Enchanted,* Gail Carson Levine (1997) (Newbery Honor). NY: Harper Trophy, a division of HarperCollins.
RL 3rd grade; **IL** 3rd–10th grade
Summary: In this Cinderella story, Ella is bewitched at birth when the mischievous fairy Lucinda bestows a gift by casting a spell of obedience. Ella is to obey all commands and not even her fairy godmother, the kitchen fairy Mandy, can remove it. After Ella's ill mother dies, her father remarries the greedy Dame Olga. Hattie, one of her two selfish stepsisters, discovers her power over Ella when she realizes that Ella must follow her commands. Ella realizes that she cannot escape her stepsister or marry the Prince, her childhood friend, because her spell would endanger his life and kingdom. Ogres, giants, elves, and gnomes add to the mystery and enchantment of this fascinating story. (232 pages)

Title: *Ghosts I Have Been,* Richard Peck (1977). NY: Puffin Books, Penguin Group.
RL 4th grade; **IL** 6th–12 grade
Summary: See Ghosts.

Title: *Harry Potter and the Sorcerer's Stone,* J. K. Rowling (1998). NY: Arthur A. Levin Books, an imprint of Scholastic Press.
RL 4th grade; **IL** 4th grade and up

Summary: The first of the popular Harry Potter series, this book describes young Harry's cruel experiences living with his heartless Uncle Vernon, selfish Aunt Petunia, and spoiled cousin Dudley. Hagrid, a sensitive giant, whisks Henry away to the Hogwarts School of Witchcraft and Wizardry, where the young wizard learns about his heritage and discovers magic, dangers, and true friendship. This is a long book (309 pages) with exotic, multisyllabic words (e.g., Voldemort, Albus Dumbledore, Hermione, Professor McGonagall), but one that has extraordinary creatures (e.g., centaurs, unicorns, trolls) and spellbinding adventures! Other books include *Harry Potter and the Chamber of Secrets, Harry Potter and the Prisoner of Azkaban,* and *Harry Potter and the Goblet of Fire.*

Title: *Holes,* Louis Sachar (1998) (National Book Award, Newbery Award). NY: Frances Foster Books, Farrar, Straus and Giroux.
RL high 3rd grade; **IL** 4th grade and up
Summary: See Adventure/Survival.

Title: *Help! I'm Trapped in My Teacher's Body!,* Todd Strasser (1993). NY: Scholastic
RL 4th grade; **IL** 4th–7th grade
Summary: Seventh grader Jake Sherman is trapped inside his "dorky" teacher's body—all due to Mr. Dirkson's ill-fated experiment to transfer intelligence in animals. A lightening storm and the science teacher's high-voltage wire switche Jake and his teacher with hilarious results. Mr. Dirkson (i.e., Jake) becomes a "cool" science teacher whereas Jake (i.e., Mr. Dirkson) discovers that his back does not hurt anymore! What happens when Ms. Rogers' feelings deepen for the new Mr. Dirkson and Jake (i.e., Mr. Dirkson) is trapped into going on a camp-out with Jake's two best friends? Will Jake and Mr. Dirkson find enough electrical wire to switch them back before a romantic dinner with Ms. Rogers? This is a laugh-aloud book that looks at multiple perspectives! (115 pages)

Title: *Help! I'm Trapped in a Vampire's Body,* Todd Strasser (2000). NY: Scholastic.
RL 4th grade; **IL** 4th–7th grade

Summary: This time Jake has his own body but a vampire lives there as well! The custodian, Vlad, a white-looking, fanged tooth man, has been trapped for 20 years with this curse. Now, thanks to Mr. Dirkson's high-voltage DITS (i.e., Dirksen Intelligence Transfer System), spilled water on the floor and a few stray wires, Jake is transformed into a boy vampire with no shadow, two long fanged teeth, and the urge to bite necks! A funny book that is a page-turner! (128 pages)

Title: *James and the Giant Peach,* Roald Dahl (1961). NY: Puffin Books, Viking Penguin.

RL 4th grade; **IL** 3rd–7th grade

Summary: James, orphaned after his parents were eaten by an angry rhinoceros who had escaped from the London Zoo, lives with his two mean aunts, Aunt Sponge and Aunt Spiker. One day James meets a little man who gives him magic green crystals. When James accidentally drops them under a peach tree, a giant peach grows and rolls away squashing the two greedy aunts. James and Old Green Grasshopper, Ladybug, Earthworm, and Centipede, insects living inside the peach, head out to sea and to adventure! (119 pages)

Title: *Just Ella,* Margaret Peterson Haddix (1999) (ALA Quick Picks for Reluctant Young Adult Readers). NY: Simon and Schuster.

RL low 5th grade; **IL** 6th grade and up

Summary: The author continues the Cinderella story when 15-year-old Ella (Cinder Ella) moves into the castle to marry Prince Charming. Ella discovers that her fantasy romance is a nightmare. The Prince is handsome, but selfish and boring, and wants only to marry a beautiful princess and have beautiful children. When Ella refuses to marry the Prince she is kept captive in the dungeon. Ella discovers a way to escape; and with the help of a kind servant girl, she digs her way out to freedom, adventure, and romance. The author writes an exciting story of intrigue and court power. Margaret Haddix has won a variety of awards that include the International Reading Association Children's Book Award, ALA Best Books for Young Adults, and ALA Quick Picks for Reluctant Young Adult Readers. (185 pages)

Title: *Midnight Magic,* Avi (1999). NY: Scholastic Press.
RL low 5th grade; **IL** 4th–9th grade
Summary: See Ghosts.

Title: *Maniac Magee,* Jerry Spinelli (1990) (Newbery Award). Boston: Little Brown and Company.
RL 4th grade; **IL** 4th–9th grade
Summary: See Adventure/Survival.

Title: *Poppy,* Avi (1996) (ALA Notable Book, a Booklist Editors' Choice). NY: Avon Books.
RL 4th grade; **IL** 4th–8th grade
Summary: Poppy is a small forest mouse who must save her family and herself from the great horned owl, Mr. Ocax, who watches over Dimwood Forest. Why is it that Mr. Ocax will not allow the forest mice to move to New House at the edge of Dimwood Forest? Only the owl can grant permission; and Poppy's romantic Ragweed pays the price for defying the powerful, menacing owl. Forest characters, like the humorous porcupine Ereth who secretly loves the gentle forest mouse, come alive under Avi's magic touch. (158 pages)

Title: *Running Out of Time,* Margaret Peterson Haddix (1995). NY: Simon and Schuster.
RL 4th grade; **IL** 3th–8th grade
Summary: Jessie and her family live in Clinton, a frontier village, in 1840. Unbeknownst to Jessie, it is really 1996, and the village she lives in is part of a tourist village where outsiders peer in to see what life in 1840 is really like! Jessie's parents and other adults consented to this experimental style of living when they became disillusioned with life in the 20th century. Now diphtheria has caused one child to die and others are sick, including Jessie's sister. The only chance for survival is for someone to escape into the 20th century to return with medicine that will stop the epidemic. Jessie's mother begs Jessie to leave Clinton; and once Jessie is in the outside world, she discovers a plot to keep her silenced. The frontier village, once created for its historical significance, has become a front for experimentation and greed. This story is an exciting page-turner! (184 pages)

Title: *Scare School, the Nightmare Room* (series), R. L. Stine (2001). NY: Avon, HarperCollins.

RL 2nd grade; **IL** 3rd–7th grade

Summary: Sam is starting at Wilton Middle School after being kicked out of his old school for fighting. On his first day at Wilton he meets a green, ugly, hairy creature in the hallway and a silent teacher and classmates. He later discovers that the school is inhabited by an imp who can do evil and harmful things, especially to new students! How can he trick the imp and free the school of this dangerous presence? The reader will discover that there is more than one imp and that Sam is the hero that won't run away! This is the 11th book in the *Nightmare Room* series. (132 pages)

Title: *Something Upstairs,* Avi (1997). NY: Avon Books.

RL middle 4th grade; **IL** 3rd–7th grade

Summary: See Mystery.

Title: *The Ghost Belonged to Me,* Richard Peck (1975). NY: Puffin, Penguin Group.

RL high 3rd grade; **IL** 4th–8th grade

Summary: See Ghosts.

Title: *The Haunting Hour: Chills in the Dead of the Night,* R. L. Stine (2001). NY: Parachute Press, HarperCollins.

RL 2nd grade; **IL** 3rd–9th grade

Summary: See Ghosts.

Title: *The Secrets of Droon: Under the Serpent Sea,* Tony Abbott (2001). NY: Scholastic.

RL 3rd grade; **IL** 2nd–5th grade

Summary: Friends Eric, Julie, and Neal return once more to the magical land of Droon to help their young friend, princess Keeah. They must obtain the Red Eye of Dawn, a magic jewel created by the evil Lord Sparr that controls the forces of nature. The young princess, who has good and angry wizard arts (the latter given to her by her aunt, the Witch Demither), travels with her friends to the realm under the Serpent Seat where danger and evil wait them! This is the 13th book in this fantasy series. (113 pages)

Title: *Tom, Babette, & Simon: Three Tales of Transformation,* Avi (1995). NY: Avon Books.

RL 4th grade; **IL** 3rd–7th grade

Summary: All three short stories describe transformations. In the first story twelve-year-old Tom is bored with his life. One day he meets and befriends Charlie, a cat. It doesn't seem strange to Tom that Charlie can talk. After a little gentle persuasion, Charlie talks Tom into changing places with him. The only problem arises when Tom tires of being a cat and longs for his home and school friends, and Charlie will not change places with him! A strange twist adds suspense to this eerie story. In the second story, Babette, an invisible, flawless daughter, longs to be seen. The third story is about Simon, a spoiled, only child who leaves home to become famous at everyone's expense. His wish is that everyone admires him. This proves to be fateful when Simon becomes trapped in his transformation—a man with a bird's head. This is a haunting tale with an important theme. (100 pages, each story about 33 pages)

Title: *Wayside School Gets a Little Stranger,* Louis Sachar (1995). NY: Avon Books.

RL 4th grade; **IL** 3rd–8th grade

Summary: See Humor.

FRIENDSHIP

PICTURE BOOKS

Title: *Chicken Sunday,* Patricia Polacco (1992). NY: Putnam & Grosset Group.

RL 3rd grade; **IL** 1st–5th grade

Summary: The author/illustrator describes her childhood friendship with neighbors Stewart and Winston and their grandmother, Miss Eula. When the three are suspected of throwing eggs at Mr. Kodinski's hat shop, they prove their innocence by decorating Russian eggs for the hat shop owner to sell. The children hope to earn enough money to buy Miss Eula the Easter hat that she has admired in Mr. Kodinski's window. This touching story celebrates Russian, Jewish, Protestant, and

African American customs and describes a special friendship between three children. (28 pages)

Title: *Smoky Night*, Eve Bunting, illustrated by David Diaz (1994) (Caldecott Award). NY: Harcourt Brace & Company.

RL high 1st, low 2nd grade; **IL** 1st–6th grade

Summary: Rioting, looting, and an apartment fire force building tenants to leave their homes and gather in a shelter. Daniel cannot find his cat (Jasmine) and Mrs. Kim has lost her cat as well. Daniel's mother and Mrs. Kim do not speak because each thinks the other is different. When a firefighter finds the two cats huddled together under the stairs, Daniel's mother and Mrs. Kim realize that they can also be friends. Full-page colorful illustrations support Bunting's important message. (25 pages)

Title: *Yo! Yes?*, Chris Raschka (1993) (Caldecott Honor). NY: Orchard Books.

RL not applicable; **IL** K–3rd grade

Summary: In only 34 one-syllable words, the author masterfully tells the story of the budding friendship between a lonely Caucasian boy and an African American boy who greets him with a smile. (23 pages)

EASY READING/SHORT CHAPTER BOOKS

Title: *A Mouse Called Wolf*, Dick King-Smith (1997). NY: Crown Publishers, a division of Random House.

RL 2nd grade; **IL** 2nd–5th grade

Summary: See Fantasy.

Title: *In Aunt Lucy's Kitchen—The Cobble Street Cousins*, Cynthia Rylant (1998). NY: Alldin Paperpacks.

RL middle 2nd grade; **IL** 2nd–5th grade

Summary: See Family Relationships.

Title: *Shoeshine Girl*, C. Bulla (1975), illustrated by J. Burke (2000). NY: Harper Trophy, HarperCollins Children's Books.

RL low 2nd grade; **IL** 2nd–5th grade
Summary: See Identity/Solving Problems.

Title: *Summer Party—The Cobble Street Cousins,* by Cynthia Rylant (2001). NY: Simon & Schuster Books for Young Readers, an imprint of Simon & Schuster Children's Publishing Division.
RL middle 2nd grade; **IL** 2nd–5th grade
Summary: See Family Relationships.

FICTION

Title: *Baseball in April and Other Short Stories,* Gary Soto (1990) (ALA Best Book for Young Adults). NY: Harcourt.
RL middle 5th grade; **IL** 3rd–7th grade
Summary: See Immigrants.

Title: *Bluish,* Virginia Hamilton (1999). NY: The Blue Sky Press, an imprint of Scholastic.
RL low 3rd grade; **IL** 3rd–7th grade
Summary: See Identity/Solving Problems.

Title: *Brian's Return,* Gary Paulsen ((1999). NY: Delacorte Press.
RL low 5th grade; **IL** 4th–9th grade
Summary: See Adventure/Survival.

Title: *Claudia's Big Party—The Baby-Sitters Club,* Ann M. Martin (1998). NY: Apple Paperbacks, Scholastic.
RL 4th grade; **IL** 3rd–7th grade
Summary: Claudia has repeated 7th grade to catch up on her grades. Now she has been transferred to 8th grade but has made new 7th grade friends and has a 7th grade boyfriend, Josh. Torn between her 8th grade Baby-Sitter Club friends, her 7th grade friends, Josh, and her schoolwork, Claudia plans a party to bring her two sets of friends together. Her older sister Janine will be the chaperone. When word gets around that Claudia is having a party, more than 12 invited guests show up! (140 pages)

Title: *Maniac Magee,* Jerry Spinelli (1990) (Newbery Award). Boston: Little Brown and Company.
RL 4th grade; **IL** 4th–9th grade
Summary: See Adventure/Survival.

Title: *Scorpions,* Walter Dean Myers (1988) (Newbery Honor Book). NY: Harper Trophy/HarperCollins.
RL high 3rd grade; **IL** 5th–10th grade
Summary: See Identity/Solving Problems.

Title: *Slam,* Walter Dean Myers (1996) (Coretta Scott King Award). NY: Scholastic Press.
RL middle to high 4th grade; **IL** 5th grade and up
Summary: See Identity/Solving Problems.

Title: *Stone Fox,* John Reynolds Gardiner (1980). NY: Harper Trophy, a division of HarperCollins.
RL 3rd grade; **IL** 4th grade and up
Summary: See Adventure/Survival.

Title: *Superfudge,* Judy Blume (1980). NY: Bantam Doubleday Dell.
RL low 4th grade; **IL** 3rd–7th grade
Summary: See Humor.

Title: *Taking Sides,* Gary Soto (1991). NY: Harcourt Brace & Company.
RL high 4th grade; **IL** 6th–10th grade
Summary: See Identity/Solving Problems.

Title: *The Skin I'm In,* Sharon Flake (1998) (Coretta Scott King Award, 1999 ALA Quick Pick for Reluctant Young Adult Readers, 1999 ALA Best Book for Young Adults). NY: Jump at the Sun, Hyperion Paperbacks for Children.
RL middle 3rd grade; **IL** 7th grade and up
Summary: See Identity/Solving Problems.

Title: *The Skirt,* Gary Soto (1992). NY: Bantam Doubleday Dell.
RL 4th grade; **IL** 3rd–6th grade
Summary: See Immigrants.

GHOSTS

EASY READING/SHORT CHAPTER BOOKS

Title: *Ghost Town at Sundown,* Mary Pope Osborne (1997) (Magic Tree House Series). NY: Random House.
RL 2nd grade; **IL** 1st–4th grade
Summary: See Mystery.

Title: *In a Dark, Dark Room and Other Scary Stories,* retold by Alvin Schwartz (1984) (An I Can Read Book). NY: HarperCollins Publisher.
RL low 1st grade; **IL** 1st–4th grade
Summary: The author retells seven scary folk tales from Europe and America. Short sentences and easy vocabulary don't interfere with these ghostly tales! The illustrations are spooky as well! (60 pages)

Title: *More Scary Stories to Tell in the Dark,* retold by Alvin Schwartz (1984). NY: Harper and Row.
RL 4th grade; **IL** 4th and up.
Summary: This is a collection of short stories that will make your hair stand on end! Titles like "Something was Wrong," "The Cat's Paw," "The Dead Man's Hand," and "A Ghost in the Mirror" give you a clue as to the scary contents. In the "notes" at the end of the book, Schwartz tells about the history surrounding the haunting tales. The drawings by Stephen Gammell are as gruesome as the folklore! (80 pages, excluding notes)

FICTION

Title: *Ghosts I Have Been,* Richard Peck (1977). NY: Puffin Books, Penguin Group.
RL 4th grade; **IL** 6th–12th grade

Summary: Fourteen-year-old Blossom Culp has the Second Sight or Psychic Gifts. She is visited by young Julian Poindexter, a tormented ghost who was a victim of the Titanic, and witnesses his abandonment by his greedy, frightened parents. When she experiences the sinking of the doomed ship along with Julian, Blossom becomes a celebrity. Newspapers quickly spread the story throughout the country and abroad. Julian's mother survives (his father is drowned) and lies to the Queen about her fortune to secure a lofty court position. Reading about Blossom's account of poor Julian's drowning and his parents' crafty, cowardly deeds, the Queen invites Blossom to visit England as her guest, along with her friends Miss Dabney and Alexander Armsworth. Only at the very end of this humorous, spooky, and mysterious tale do we discover whether Julian's tormented spirit is finally put to rest. (This book follows the author's ghost story *The Ghost Belonged to Me* that is described in this section). (214 pages)

Title: *Midnight Magic,* Avi (1999) (ALA Quick Picks for Reluctant Young Adult Readers). NY: Scholastic Press.

RL low 5th grade; **IL** 4th–9th grade

Summary: Mangus, the magician, and his faithful servant boy Fabrizio have been summoned by the King to prove or disprove the "ghost" that princess Teresina vows is haunting her. According to the frightened princess, the ghost is the spirit of her brother that has been murdered by the evil Count Scarazoni. Court intrigue, attempted murder, deception and magic are all part of this fascinating story set in the Middle Ages. (249 pages)

Title: *Pets,* Avi (1997). In *What Do Fish Have to Do with Anything?* (pp. 119–148). Cambridge, MA: Candlewick Press.

RL 3rd grade; **IL** 3rd–7th grade

Summary: Eve loves pets. After her dog Chase dies of old age, she receives two kittens from her parents, feisty Angel and gentle Shadow. She is heartbroken when Angel dies of distemper, and Shadow is soon to follow. One evening Eve notices the cats on her bed, enticing her to follow them, feed them, and become their pet! When she becomes very ill, and the cats are scratching at her, pulling her away to join them, her only hope is Chase. This is an eerie ghost story with a surprising resolution! (29 pages in a fascinating short story collection)

Title: *Something Upstairs,* Avi (1997). NY: Avon Books.
RL middle 4th grade; **IL** 3rd–7th grade
Summary: See Mystery.

Title: *The Ghost Belonged to Me,* Richard Peck (1975). NY: Puffin, Penguin Group.
RL high 3rd grade; **IL** 4th–8th grade
Summary: The time is 1913 and 13-year-old Alexander notices candle light beaming from the barn. Blossom, a headstrong classmate, tells Alexander that her mother says that he has the "Gift" (being receptive to the Spirit World). And indeed he has when he comes face-to-face with Inez Dumaine, a drowning victim with wet petticoats and a sad, haunting face that warns him of an upcoming disaster. Alexander becomes a hero, saving lives from a grisly trolley car accident, yet has to admit that a ghost warned him! Alexander's eccentric and colorful Uncle Miles has more to add to Inez' sad story and Blossom is instrumental in providing peace for the young, troubled ghost. The author's humor and ghostly plot make this a fun, page-turner. (159 pages)

Title: *The Haunting Hour: Chills in the Dead of the Night,* R. L. Stine (2001). NY: Parachute Press, HarperCollins Publishing.
RL 2nd grade; **IL** 3rd–9th grade
Summary: Ten new short stories captivate readers with ghostly tales of Egyptian mummies, a sinister baby-sitter who bakes dangerous mud cookies, and Halloween ghouls that leave their tombs to dance on Halloween. Surprise endings are more common than not in these scary tales laced with a dash of humor. Stories range from 18 to 20 pages. (153 pages)

HISTORICAL FICTION

PICTURE BOOKS

Title: *Gleam and Glow,* Eve Bunting (2001). NY: Harcourt.
RL 2nd grade; **IL** 1st–6th grade
Summary: See Family Relationships.

Title: *Minty: A Story of Young Harriet Tubman,* Alan Schroeder, illustrations by Jerry Pinkney (1996). NY: Dial Books for Young Readers, a division of Penguin Books.

RL 2nd grade; **IL** all ages

Summary: Young Harriet Tubman is a slave on the Brodas plantation where she is frequently punished for her headstrong ways. Telling her father that she is going to run away someday, he teaches her to look for the North Star, how to survive in the forest, catch fish, and light a fire. Although Minty doesn't escape in this story, the author notes that she eventually escapes from the Brodas' plantation and helps countless others find their way to freedom by way of the Underground Railroad. Jerry Pinkney's realistic, vivid watercolors inspire emotions that support this good story. (37 pages)

Title: *Pink and Say,* Patrica Polacco (1994). NY: Philomel Books, a division of the Putnam & Grosset Group.

RL 2nd grade; **IL** all ages

Summary: This moving story describes the author's great, great grandfather Sheldon Russel Curtis (Say), a young Union deserter, and Pinkus Aylee (Pink), a young slave. Both are 14 years old and fight for the Union. Pink discovers Say, a deserter, lying wounded and near death, and takes him home to be nursed by his mother, Moe Moe Bay. After Say regains his health and the boys decide to return to their outfits, Confederate soldiers storm the old house, killing Moe Moe. The young soldiers are captured but only one boy returns home. This story, based on actual events, celebrates bravery and friendship and echoes the sadness and loss of war. The author's poignant illustrations and words describe this extraordinary friendship. (40 pages)

EASY READING/SHORT CHAPTER BOOKS

Title: *Finding Providence: The Story of Roger Williams,* Avi (1997). NY: Harper Trophy, HarperCollins Children's Book.

RL high 3rd grade; **IL** 2nd–5th grade

Summary: In 1635 Roger Williams is on trial for preaching dangerous ideas—that church and government should be separated, that no one should be forced to attend church, and that Europeans have no right to take the Indians' land. Branded a traitor, Roger flees the Massachusetts Bay Colony and finds refuge with the Narragansett Indians who offer shelter to him and his family. Their home, Providence, is to become a haven for those who believe in the separation of church and state. This fascinating story is told from the point of view of Roger's daughter, Mary. (47 pages)

Title: *A Lion to Guard Us,* Clyde Bulla (1981). NY: Harper Trophy, HarperCollins Children's Books.
RL low 2nd grade; **IL** 2nd–5th grade
Summary: Based on factual events that took place in 1609 when an English ship sailing for Jamestown shipwrecked on the Bermuda Islands during a violent storm, Bulla tells the story of Amanda, her sister Meg, and brother Jemmy as they journey to Virginia to find their father. Jemmy fiercely holds on to the brass lion doorknocker that his father gave him from their family home in London when shipmates try to steal it for its falsely perceived value. The children must depend on their wit and bravery to survive greedy shipmates and the forces of nature. This easy-to-read chapter book is full of adventure. (115 pages with full-page illustrations)

Title: *Sarah, Plain and Tall,* Patricia MacLachlan (1985) (Newbery Medal). Harper Trophy, a division of HarperCollins.
RL 3rd grade; **IL** 3rd–7th grade
Summary: This gentle, moving story centers on Sarah Elisabeth Wheaton, who leaves Maine and her beloved sea to live with a widower and his two children on the prairie. She will stay one month to see how things work out. This elegant, short story is told in first person through the eyes of Anna, the daughter. (58 pages)

Title: *The Josefina Story Quilt,* Eleanor Coerr (1986) (An I Can Read Book). NY: Harper Trophy, a division of HarperCollins.
RL 2nd grade; **IL** 2nd–4th grade
Summary: Faith is traveling to California in 1850 with her parents and brother in a covered wagon loaded with pots, pans, and quilts. After begging her parents to take the old pet hen Josefina, her mother and father give in and the family and hen begin the long journey. On the

way Josefina is trouble. Frightened by a dog in the wagon train, the hen starts an animal stampede. Next she falls into the river when the wagon loses a wheel. As the family nears their destination, robbers try to steel Ma's warm quilts, but Josefina's large cackle frightens them away. This proves to be too much for the old hen that is found dead on the floor of her cage. After the family buries Josefina, Faith begins a memory quilt in honor of her faithful friend. (64 pages)

Title: *The Sword in the Tree,* Clyde Bulla (1956), illustrations by Paul Casale (2000). NY: Harper Trophy, HarperCollins Children's Book.

RL low 2nd grade; **IL** 2nd–5th grade

Summary: Lord Lionel, Shan's treacherous uncle, reports that Shan's father has fallen into quicksand on a hunting trip and has died. The devious uncle quickly becomes Lord of Weldon Castle, bringing in friends and servants to support his claim. Shan and his mother, Lady Marian, fearing for their lives, escape from the Castle and find refuge with Magnus, the son of a herdsman. Convinced by Magnus to travel to Camelot to plead for help from King Arthur, Shan is granted an audience with the King. Arthur sends Sir Garth to Weldon Castle to discover the rightful owner of Weldon Castle. A hidden sword in the hollow of an old tree reveals the truth. (103 pages)

FICTION

Title: *A Year Down Yonder,* Richard Peck (2000) (Newbery Award). NY: Dial Books for Young Readers, a division of Penguin Putnam.

RL 4th grade; **IL** 4th grade and up

Summary: See Humor.

Title: *Esperanza Rising,* Pam Muñoz Ryan (2000). NY: Scholastic Press.

RL 5th grade; **IL** 5th–8th grade

Summary: See Identity/Solving Problems.

Title: *Nightjohn,* Gary Paulsen (1993) (ALA Best Book for Young Adults, IRA Children's Choice). NY: Bantam Doubleday Dell.

RL 4th grade; **IL** 4th–9th grade

Summary: This gripping story, told from the perspective of the young slave Sarney, is about the slave Nightjohn, who risks his life to teach others to read. Although Nightjohn escapes capture, he always returns to empower others through reading. The sequel, *Sarny: A Life Remembered,* focuses on Sarny's adult life after the Civil War. (178 pages)

Title: *The Barn,* Avi (1994) (ALA Notable Book). NY: Avon Books.

RL low 5th grade; **IL** 3rd–7th grade

Summary: Nine-year-old Benjamin must leave school to return to the family farm when his father suffers a stroke-like illness that leaves him only able to blink his eyes. It is up to Benjamin, his older brother Harrison, and sister Nettie (who soon hopes to marry) to keep the farm running. It is Benjamin's idea to build a barn, a gift from the three of them that will help his father get well. Working near to exhaustion, Benjamin, Harrison, and Nettie must complete the barn before it is too late. Set in 1855, the author depicts the hardships of farming and the loyalty of family. (106 pages)

Title: *The Fighting Ground,* Avi (1984). NY: HarperCollins Children's Books

RL high 3rd grade; **IL** 3rd–7th grade

Summary: Thirteen-year-old Jonathan leaves home unbeknownst to his father and mother to fight against the British and Hessians (German mercenary soldiers) during the American Revolution. Joining the Corporal (the hard, tough leader of a small group of volunteers), Jonathan finds himself in the middle of battle, running for his life. He is captured by three Hessians and soon realizes that the soldiers will do him no harm. Jonathan and the soldiers hide in a small deserted cabin and discover a small child and his murdered parents in the nearby woods. Assuming the deaths are the work of the German soldiers, Jonathan escapes with the boy and finds the Corporal who demands that he lead the group back to the Hessians. Realizing that it is the Corporal who has murdered the child's parents (assumed traitors because they are French), Jonathan tries to warn the three sleeping Hessians. This fast-paced story reflects the ambiguity and destruction of war and a young boy's courage to try to listen to his conscience. (152 pages)

Title: *The True Confessions of Charlotte Doyle,* Avi (1990) (Newbery Honor, ALA Best Book for Young Adults). NY: Avon Camelot Book.

RL 4th grade; **IL** 3rd–8th grade

Summary: Charlotte, age 15, attends the Barrington School for Better Girls in England so that she can obtain (according to her merchant father) an appropriate education for a lady in 1832. When her father must return to America, Charlotte is to complete the school term before joining her family. She returns to America aboard the Seahawk, a ship under the control of the notorious Captain Jaggery. On her return voyage, Charlotte witnesses the Captain's cruelty; becomes a shipmate (wearing sailor's clothes); and is accused of a murder, tried, and sentenced to death. Zachariah, an old African American crew member, comes to her rescue and helps Charlotte discover what she values in life. This is an exciting story with a fast-moving plot and strong female character. (221 pages)

HUMOR

PICTURE BOOKS

Title: *A Fine, Fine School,* Sharon Creech (2001). NY: Joanna Cotler Books, HarperCollins.

RL 1st grade; **IL** K–4th grade

Summary: All of the children and teachers in Mr. Keene's school don't want to disappoint the enthusiastic principal who says that school will continue on the weekends, during the holidays, and finally, throughout the year, because it is such a fine, fine school! Only when Tille tells Mr. Keene that she doesn't have time to climb her favorite tree, push her brother on a swing, or learn to sit for an hour does the well-meaning principal see the error of his ways! Harry Bliss' humorous cartoon illustrations depict how dismayed students and teachers feel throughout Mr. Keene's exhausting school year! (29 pages)

Title: *Are You My Mother?,* P. D. Eastman (1960, 1988). NY: Random House.

RL 1st grade; **IL** K–3rd grade
Summary: A young bird hatches from his egg and, finding his mother gone, wanders off to find her. First he meets a kitten, then a hen, a dog, a cow, a car, a boat, an airplane, and a stem shovel, none of which are his mother. The steam shovel gently deposits the tiny bird in his nest. To his surprise, he sees his mother with a big worm in her mouth. Repetitive sentences and cartoon illustrations support struggling young readers as they read this humorous story. (64 pages)

Title: *Green Eggs and Ham*, Dr. Suess (1960). NY: Random House.
RL 1st grade; **IL** K–4th grade
Summary: See Fantasy.

Title: *I Like Me*, Nancy Carlson (1988). NY: Viking Kestrel, Penguin Group.
RL 1st grade; **IL** 1st–3rd grade
Summary: See Identity/Solving Problems.

Title: *Oh, the Places You'll Go!*, Dr. Suess (1990). NY: Random House.
RL 1st grade; **IL** 3rd grade and up
Summary: See Identity/Solving Problems.

Title: *The Cat in the Hat*, Dr. Suess (1957). NY: Random House.
RL 1st grade; **IL** K–3rd grade
Summary: See Fantasy.

EASY READING/SHORT CHAPTER BOOKS

Title: *Amelia Bedelia*, Peggy Parish (1963). NY: HarperCollins.
RL 2nd grade; **IL** 1st–4th grade
Summary: Amelia Bedelia's first day of work for Mr. and Mrs. Rogers turns out to be a catastrophe! Amelia interprets Mrs. Rogers' directions in a most concrete way. She "dusts" the furniture with dusting powder and "changes" the towels by cutting holes in them! Amelia bakes a meringue pie to surprise the Rogers on their return. The pie

tastes so heavenly that rather than fire Amelia, Mrs. Rogers learns to say "undust" when she means dust and makes other modifications as well. This is one of many delightful Amelia Bedelia books. (27 pages)

Title: *Aunt Eater Loves A Mystery,* Doug Cushman (1987) (An I Can Read Book). NY: Harper Trophy, a division of HarperCollins.
RL low 2nd grade; **IL** 1st–3rd grade
Summary: See Fantasy.

Title: *Detective Dinosaur Lost and Found,* James Skofield (1998) (An I Can Read Book). NY: Harper Trophy, a division of Harper-Collins.
RL low 2nd grade; **IL** 1st–3rd grade
Summary: See Fantasy.

Title: *Marvin Redpost: A Magic Crystal?,* Louis Sachar (2000). NY: Random House.
RL middle 2nd grade; **IL** 2nd–5th grade
Summary: Casey Happleton has a magic crystal that makes wishes come true and Marvin Redpost doesn't know whether to believe her or not! Easy wishes like an ice cream sundae and cookies and milk come true (did Casey make these happen?). Only when Marvin wishes that Casey would be quiet and she stops talking does he think the magic crystal might be magic. What will undo Marvin's wish? What is Marvin's last secret wish and what becomes of the magic crystal? Marvin's problems are humorously solved in this easy-to-read chapter book. (81 pages)

Title: *Marvin Redpost Alone in His Teacher's House,* Louis Sachar (1994). NY: Random House.
RL low 2nd; **IL** 1st–4th grade
Summary: Mrs. North, Marvin's' teacher, has asked Marvin to take care of her 17-year-old dog Waldo while she is away on a week's vacation. Marvin has the key to Mrs. North's house, and his friends are jealous. Plus, he is in trouble at school with the substitute through no fault of his own! The worse event is Waldo. He won't eat and after Marvin feeds him liver, he finds that the old dog has died under the bed.

What will Mrs. North do? What will Waldo do? This is a touching story about an old dog, a responsible boy, and a grateful teacher.

Title: *Marvin Redpost, Is He a Girl?*, Louis Sachar (1993). NY: Random House.
RL high 1st grade; **IL** 1st–4th grade
Summary: Casey, a know-it-all schoolmate, tells Marvin he will turn into a girl if he kisses his elbow. Trying (and not trying) to kiss his elbow, he falls out of bed in a tangle of sheets to find that he has indeed, kissed his elbow! Then things start to happen! He imagines that he thinks like a girl, talks like a girl, and appreciates how girls look and act. Now he has to discover how to undo what he thinks he did! The author writes a hilarious story about perceived differences. (71 pages)

Title: *Mouse Soup*, Arnold Lobel (1977) (An I Can Read Book). NY: Harper Trophy, a division of HarperCollins.
RL 1st grade; **IL** 1st–3rd grade
Summary: See Fantasy.

Title: *Mouse Tales*, Arnold Lobel (1972) (An I Can Read Book). NY: Harper Trophy, a division of HarperCollins.
RL 1st grade; **IL** 1st–3rd grade
Summary: See Fantasy.

Title: *Mr. Putter & Tabby Paint the Porch*, Cynthia Rylant (2000). NY: Harcourt.
RL low 2nd grade; **IL** 1st–3rd grade
Summary: This is a series that features Mr. Putter and his loving cat Tabby. Arthur Howard's gentle watercolors depict the delightful white-haired man and his pet. In this book, Mr. Putter decides to paint the porch post pink. Tabby and a squirrel end up with more paint than the post, and neighbor Mrs. Teaberry and dog Zeke get in the fray. Delightful, charming, easy-to-read stories, especially for cat lovers! (48 pages)

Title: *Poppleton in Fall*, Cynthia Rylant (1999). NY: Scholastic.
RL low 1st grade; **IL** 1st–3rd grade

Summary: See Fantasy.

Title: *Poppleton in Spring,* Cynthia Rylant (1999). NY: Scholastic.
RL low 1st grade; **IL** 1st–3rd grade
Summary: See Fantasy.

Title: *The Golly Sisters Go West,* Betsy Byars (1985) (An I Can Read Book). NY: HarperTrophy.
RL 1st grade; **IL** 1st–3rd grade
Summary: The zanny sisters May-May and Rose go out West to entertain settlers with their singing and dancing. On the way the sisters have hilarious mishaps that the illustrator, Sue Truesdell, captures in funny, comic-style watercolors. Betsy Byars, award-winning author, uses short, repetitious sentences to cleverly portray these unusual western gals! Other books include *The Golly Sisters Ride Again* and *Hurray for the Golly Sisters.* (64 pages)

Title: *The Imp That Ate My Homework!,* Lawrence Yep (1998). NY: Harper Trophy, a division of HarperCollins.
RL 2nd grade; **IL** 3rd–7th grade
Summary: See Fantasy.

Title: *The Time Warp Trio, It's All Greek to Me,* Jon Scieszka (1999). NY: Puffin Books.
RL 2nd grade; **IL** 2nd–6th grade
Summary: See Fantasy.

Title: *The Zack Files,* Dan Greenburg (2000). NY: Grosset & Dunlap.
RL middle 2nd grade; **IL** 2nd–5th grade
Summary: See Fantasy.

POETRY

Title: *If Pigs Could Fly . . . And Other Deep Thoughts,* Bruce Lansky (2000). NY: Meadowbrook Press, distributed by Simon & Simon.
RL not applicable; **IL** 1st–6th grade
Summary: See Poetry.

Title: *Insect Soup: Bug Poems,* Barry Louis Polisar (1999). Silver Spring, MD: Rainbow Morning Music.
RL not applicable; **IL** 1st–5th grade
Summary: See Poetry.

Title: *No More Homework! No More Tests! Kids Favorite Funny School Poems,* selected by Bruce Lansky (1997). NY: Meadowbrook Press, distributed by Simon & Simon.
RL not applicable; **IL** 1st–6th grade
Summary: See Poetry.

FICTION

Title: *A Year Down Yonder,* Richard Peck (2000) (Newbery Medal). NY: Dial Books for Young Readers, a division of Penguin Putnam.
RL 4th grade; **IL** 4th grade and up
Summary: Mary Alice, 15, must spend the year with Grandma in a "hick town" because of hard times. It is 1937 and because her father has lost his job, the family must move from their Chicago apartment into a smaller place, only big enough for her parents. Her brother Joey has a job out west, and Mary Alice must live with Grandma until her family gets settled again. After a year of exciting and hilarious adventures with her eccentric Grandma (e.g., hosting a stuffy meeting with her spiked punch and secret guests, housing a snake in the rafters that terrifies a new lodger, and avenging the Halloween night tricksters), Mary Alice doesn't want to go home! This is the sequel to *A Long Way from Chicago,* a Newbery Honor Book. (130 pages)

Title: *Bunnicula: A Rabbit-Tale of Mystery,* Deborah and James Howe (1979). NY: Avon Books.
RL 3rd grade; **IL** 3rd–7th grade
Summary: Told in first person through the eyes of Harold, the easygoing, friendly, family dog, this funny story describes the perils of Bunnicula, a bunny that the family finds in a movie theater and brings home as a pet. Chester, the jealous and rather neurotic family cat, believes Bunnicula is a vampire and dreams up all sorts of mischievous ways to reveal the small rabbit's true persona. Harold comes to Bun-

nicula's rescue and saves the harmless bunny from Chester's scheming plans. (98 pages)

Title: *Bunnicula Strikes Again!*, James Howe (1999). NY: Atheneum Books, an imprint of Simon & Schuster Children's Publishing Division.

RL middle 4th grade; **IL** 3rd–7th grade

Summary: Chester, the family cat, is again out to trap Bunnicula. This time, the puppy Howie (Harold's young nephew) and Harold must move quickly to save the innocent bunny. But in the end, when both rabbit and cat are trapped under rubble from the demolition of the movie theater (showing the film *Dracula*), a surprising event occurs that is reported on the evening news and ends up on the front page of the newspaper! (116 pages)

Title: *Freckle Juice*, Judy Blume (1971). NY: Bantam Doubleday Dell.

RL 2nd grade; **IL** 1st–4th grade

Summary: Andrew is always late for school because he has to wash behind his neck! If he had freckles his mother would never know if his neck needed washing or not! Nicky Lane has freckles all over his face and neck; and Andrew wants freckles, too. Sharon, a prissy, know-it-all classmate, has a secret recipe for freckle juice that she will sell for 50 cents. Andrew takes the bait, and the fun begins! A short, hilarious story! (47 pages)

Title: *Help! I'm Trapped in My Teacher's Body!*, Todd Strasser (1993). NY: Scholastic.

RL low 4th grade; **IL** 4th–7th grade

Summary: See Fantasy.

Title: *Help! I'm Trapped in a Vampire's Body*, Todd Strasser (2000). Scholastic.

RL low 4th grade; **IL** 4th–7th grade

Summary: See Fantasy.

Title: *How to Eat Fried Worms*, Thomas Rockwell (1973). NY: Dell Publishing Company.

RL middle 2nd grade; **IL** 2nd–7th grade

Summary: Alan bets Billy 50 dollars that he can't eat a worm a day for 15 days! There are rules: Billy can eat them any way he wants (e.g., boiled, stewed, fried, fricasseed), but Alan and friend Joe must provide the worms. This humorous story gets funnier as Billy's family gets involved, all eating *Alsatian Smothered Worm,* a dish that Billy's mother finds in her French cookbook! (116 pages)

Title: *Love That Dog,* Sharon Creech (2001). NY: Joanna Cotler Books, HarperCollins.

RL 2nd grade; **IL** 3rd–7th grade

Summary: Jack, a student in Miss Stretchberry's class, doesn't think that he can write poetry; but when he follows the writing style of poet Walter Dean Myers, he discovers that he can be a writer! (Walter Dean Myers' "Love That Boy" inspires Jack's "Love That Dog.") This humorous, easy-to-read book, written from Jack's point of view, describes his writing journey and unexpected encounter with the famous Walter Dean Myers. (86 pages)

Title: *Superfudge,* Judy Blume (1980). NY: Bantam Doubleday Dell.

RL low 4th grade; **IL** 3rd–7th grade

Summary: Much to his dismay, Peter finds out that his four-year-old brother Fudge and parents are moving from their New York City apartment to Princeton for a year and that his mom is going to have a baby! Once in Princeton and in the 6th grade, Peter makes a new friend (Alex), discovers that he can still be best friends with his old friend (Jimmy), and finds a girlfriend (in classmate Joanne). Fudge has his own problems when he enters kindergarten and his "rat-faced" teacher refuses to call him Fudge! Family relationships, friendship, and humor are all part of this funny, warm-hearted story. (166 pages)

Title: *Wayside School Gets a Little Stranger,* Louis Sachar (1995). NY: Avon Books.

RL 4th grade; **IL** 3rd–8th grade

Summary: A 30-story school building with a single classroom on each floor, weird teachers, and strange events greet wary students as they begin the school year in Wayside School! Be sure to read Sachar's other hilarious Wayside School books, *Sideways Stories from Wayside School* and *Wayside School is Falling Down*. (168 pages)

IDENTITY/SOLVING PROBLEMS

PICTURE BOOKS

Title: *I Like Me!*, Nancy Carlson (1988). NY: Viking Kestrel, Penguin Group.
RL 1st grade; **IL** K–3rd grade
Summary: A smiling little pig is quite pleased with herself! Colorful illustrations and short, simple sentences describe the many ways in which the beaming pig thinks she is quite swell! This is a delightful, humorous picture book that addresses self-concept. (30 pages)

Title: *Oh, the Places You'll Go!*, Dr. Seuss (1990). NY: Random House.
RL 1st grade; **IL** 3rd grade and up
Summary: Short rhyming verse and whimsical, fantasy illustrations describe the ups and downs and scary, exciting places of finding one's way through life. This wonderful book is sure to inspire and give courage to meet problems and grapple with challenges! (44 pages)

Title: *Thank you, Mr. Falker,* Patricia Polacco (1998). NY: Philomel Books, a division of the Putnam & Grosset Group.
RL 3rd grade; **IL** 1st–5th grade
Summary: Trisha cannot read; and now that she has moved to a new school, classmates make fun of her and call her "dummy." Mr. Falker, the new 5th grade teacher, raves about Trisha's brilliant drawing and dicovers Trisha's secret when she helps him clean erasers after school. With the help of Mr. Falker and the reading teacher, Trisha learns to unlock the mystery of written symbols. This moving, autobiographical story about this distinguished author/illustrator reinforces the importance of celebrating strengths and providing individual support for children with reading difficulties. (35 pages)

Title: *Wings,* Christopher Myers (2000). NY: Scholastic Press.
RL low 4th grade; **IL** all ages
Summary: Ikarus Jackson is different. He can fly. Classmates, except for one shy, quiet girl, make fun of his wings; and the teacher says that because of him no one can pay attention. Finally, gathering up her courage, the girl tells him that his flying is beautiful. Ikarus soars in the clouds with a smile on his face. This beautifully illustrated and written picture book fantasy celebrates friendship and differences. (38 pages)

EASY READING/SHORT CHAPTER BOOKS

Title: *Shoeshine Girl,* Clyde Bulla (1975), illustrated by J. Burke (2000). NY: Harper Trophy, HarperCollins Children's Books.
RL low 2nd grade; **IL** 2nd–5th grade
Summary: Sarah Ida, 10-1/2 years of age, reluctantly visits her Aunt Claudia during the summer in the small town of Palmville. She is at odds with everyone (parents included) and feels that no one listens to or cares about her. When Sarah Ida wants to have money in her pocket, she finds that the only way is to work in Al's shoeshine stand as a "shoeshine girl." A friendship blossoms and when Al is hit by a car, and Sarah Ida finds that she is dependable. Wanting to help Al, she keeps the stand open by shining shoes and discovers the importance of responsibility, friendship, and loyalty. (84 pages)

Title: *The Skirt,* Gary Soto (1992). NY: Bantam Doubleday Dell.
RL 4th grade; **IL** 4th–7th grade
Summary: See Immigrants.

NONFICTION

Title: *I Can't Accept Not Trying: Michael Jordan on the Pursuit of Excellence,* Michael Jordan (1994). NY: HarperCollins.
RL 4th grade; **IL** 4th–9th grade
Summary: See Sports.

Title: *Roberto Clemente,* James Buckley, Jr. (2001). NY: Dorling Kindersley Readers.

RL 6th grade; **IL** all ages
Summary: See Sports.

Title: *Shoot for the Moon: The Amazing Life and Times of Annie Oakley,* Stephen Krensky (2001). NY: Melanie Kroupa Books, Farrar, Straus and Giroux.
RL 3rd grade; **IL** all ages
Summary: See Biography.

FICTION

Title: *An Island Like You: Stories of the Barrio,* Judith Ortiz Cofer (1995) (ALA Best Book for Young Adults, Pura Belpre Award). NY: Puffin Books.
RL 5th grade; **IL** 7th–12th grade
Summary: Twelve short stories describe the hopes, fears, and friendships of teenagers such as Arturo, Sandra, Luis, Teresa, and Rita, whose parents or close relatives have immigrated to the United States from Puerto Rico. The teenagers all have their own story that reflects the struggles and satisfaction from growing up and living in the barrio, a Hispanic community in Paterson, New Jersey. (165 pages, each short story is about 25 pages)

Title: *Baseball in April and Other Short Stories,* Gary Soto (1990) (ALA Best Book for Young Adults). NY: Harcourt.
RL middle 5th grade; **IL** 3rd–7th grade
Summary: A collection of short stories about children whose parents or grandparents are immigrants from Mexico. The realistic stories depict everyday experiences in the lives of Alfonso, Michael, Jessie, Veronica, Manual, and others. The author includes Spanish words and phrases and their English translations. (107 pages)

Title: *Blackwater,* Eve Bunting (1999) (2000 ALA Quick Picks for Reluctant Young Adult Readers). NY: Harper Troper/HarerCollins Publishers.
RL middle 2nd grade; **IL** 5th grade and up
Summary: Thirteen-year-old Brodie takes his troublesome cousin

Alex to the Blackwater River to learn how to swim. Between the pond and the river is a giant rock called the "Toadstool" that separates the river's dangerous rapids from the shallow water. Brodie recognizes Pauline (whom he likes) laughing with Otis McCandless on the Toadstool. He swims out to tease Pauline and causes the two to fall backwards, into the swirling river. Frantically trying to help them, Brodie realizes that they have been swept away by the rapids. Alex persuades Brodie to keep quiet about his involvement in the tragedy when Pauline's body is found and Otis is missing. This is a powerful, gripping story about right and wrong, the consequences of telling a lie, and the importance of family. (146 pages)

Title: *Bluish,* Virginia Hamilton (1999). NY: The Blue Sky Press, an imprint of Scholastic.
RL low 3rd grade; **IL** 3rd–7th grade
Summary: A moving story about the relationship between Dreenie; her friend Tuli; and Natalie, called "Bluish," because of her transparent, blue–white skin caused by leukemia. At first afraid that she will get Natalie's illness, Dreenie avoids the new 5th grader. When Dreenie accepts Natalie's invitation to visit her home after school, the barriers dissolve as Dreenie learns that Natalie is much like herself. Dreenie, and then Tuli, develop a strong friendship with Bluish that is heartwarming, sometimes humorous, and uplifting. (127 pages)

Title: *Brian's Return,* Gary Paulsen (1999). NY: Delacorte Press.
RL low 5th grade; **IL** 4th–9th grade
Summary: See Adventure/Survival.

Title: *Brian's Winter,* Gary Paulsen (1996). NY: Delacorte Press.
RL low 5th grade; **IL** 4th–9th grade
Summary: See Adventure/Survival.

Title: *Esperanza Rising,* Pam Muñoz Ryan (2000). NY: Scholastic Press.
RL 5th grade; **IL** 5th–9th grade
Summary: Esperanza and her parents live on El Rancho de la Rosa, a prosperous Mexican ranch in 1930. Her father is a wealthy landowner

who is tragically killed by bandits the day before Esperanza's 13th birthday. When Esperanza's greedy uncle takes over the land and burns the ranch, Esperanza and her mother escape with farm workers (Hortensia, Alfonso, and their son Miguel) to the farm labor camps in California. Esperanza no longer has the privileged life she was used to and experiences hardships, backbreaking work, discrimination, and her mother's near-death. With Miguel's help, Esperanza comes to realize that the greatest wealth does not come from money or position. (253 pages)

Title: *Hatchet,* Gary Paulsen (1987). NY: Puffin Books.
RL low 5th grade; **IL** 4th–9th grade
Summary: See Adventure/Survival.

Title: *Joey Pigza Loses Control,* Jack Gantos (2000) (Newbery Honor Book). NY: Farrar, Straus and Giroux.
RL low 4th grade; **IL** 4th–7th grade
Summary: Joey and his dog Pablo visit Joey's father during summer vacation. His parents are divorced and his mother has misgivings about the visit. Joey, on medication for his hyperactivity but definitely in control, has hopes for a reunited family. When Joey's dad takes away his patches to teach him independence, Joey realizes that he is getting out of control, and that his dad, who drinks too much and is hyper himself, needs more help than he does. This sensitive story is told through Joey's point of view. (196 pages)

Title: *Joey Pigza Swallowed the Key,* Jack Gantos (1998) (ALA Notable Children's Book). NY: Harper Trophy, HarperCollins.
RL high 3rd grade; **IL** 4th–7th grade
Summary: Joey is wired like his grandmother and father. His attention disorder prevents him from sitting still. After a series of mishaps, including swallowing his house key and tripping with a pair of scissors in his hands causing him to cut a classmate's nose, he is sent to a "special ed." school. There he makes friends, receives new medication, and discovers that he is really a good kid! This story precedes Joey Pigza Loses Control. (154 pages)

Title: *Maniac Magee,* Jerry Spinelli (1990) (Newbery Award). Boston: Little Brown and Company.
RL 4th grade; **IL** 4th–9th grade
Summary: See Adventure/Survival.

Title: *Monster,* Walter Dean Myers (1999) (National Book Award Finalist, Michael L. Printz Award, ALA Quick Picks for Reluctant Young Adult Readers). NY: HarperCollins.
RL low 4th grade; **IL** 6th grade and up
Summary: Sixteen-year-old Steve Harmon is on trial for a murder that occurred during a drug store robbery. To survive Cell Block D, Manhattan Detention Center, Steve writes a screenplay of the trial. He calls his play *Monster,* to reflect his perception of himself as well as that of the prosecuting attorney. The story is structured around Steve's play (characters, setting, dialogue) and his tormented diary notes. This is a powerful, gripping story of how one night, a bad choice, and dangerous friends can change tomorrow. The suspenseful story leaves the reader with much to think about. (281 pages)

Title: *Seedfolks,* Paul Fleischman (1997) (ALA Best Books for Young Adults, ALA Quick Picks for Young Adults, 1998 IRA Children's Choices). NY: HarperCollins.
RL high 3rd grade; **IL** 5th grade and up
Summary: See Immigrants.

Title: *Scorpions,* Walter Dean Myers (1988) (Newbery Honor Book). NY: Harper Trophy/HarperCollins.
RL high 3rd to low 4th grade; **IL** 5th–10th grade
Summary: Jamal's older brother Randy is in jail for robbery, and Jamal is asked to lead his brother's gang, the Scorpions. When Crazy Mack gives Jamal a gun, it is Tito, Jamal's gentle Puerto Rican friend, who tries to protect him. This is a moving story about family, friendship, and the conflict that 12-year-old Jamal faces as he tries to help his mother, support his brother Randy and the gang, and be true to himself and his best friend. (216 pages)

Title: *Slam,* Walter Dean Myers (1996) (Coretta Scott King Award). NY: Scholastic Press.

RL middle to high 4th grade; **IL** 5th grade and up

Summary: Greg Harris, known as "Slam" because of his slam dunks on the court, is in trouble with the coach. Rather than take orders, Slam wants to play the game his way. He also is having trouble in school and discovers that his best friend may be involved in drugs. This is a quick-paced story about friendship, discipline, holding on to strengths, and discovering one's identity on and off the court. (266 pages)

Title: *Taking Sides,* Gary Soto (1991). NY: Harcourt Brace & Company.

RL high 4th grade; **IL** 6th–10th grade

Summary: Lincoln Mendoza has recently moved to a more affluent, mostly white suburb because his mother wants to be free of the crime and hardship of living in the city. Lincoln misses his good friend Tony and his Franklin basketball team; and he realizes that Columbus Coach Yesutis has it in for him because he is Mexican and comes from Franklin, a team that the coach lost to years ago while playing on an opposing team. Columbus will play Franklin in an important school game, and Lincoln must play against his friends if Coach Yesutis allows him to play at all. Although Lincoln has made good friends in his new school (Eric, who is white; and Monica, who is also Mexican American), he misses his old friends and has conflicting feelings about who he is and where he belongs. Warmly greeted by his old Franklin coach and Franklin teammates, Lincoln realizes that he can maintain his friends from Franklin and Columbus junior high while living in the suburbs. Spanish phrases are interspersed throughout the book with a glossary at the end for Spanish words and phrases. (135 pages)

Title: *The Landry News,* Andrew Clements (1999). NY: Aladdin Paperbacks.

RL 5th grade; **IL** 3rd–8th grade

Summary: Cara is a new girl in Mr. Larson's 5th grade class. Having recently moved after her parent's divorce, Cara is a loner and likes it that way. She discovers that Mr. Larson's class is easy! He doesn't teach! After he gets the class started on worksheets or story writing, the once "Teacher of the Year" goes back to his paper and thermos of cold coffee. He use to be a good teacher but somehow has slipped into a rut with his "open classroom" philosophy. Cara, who wants to be a newspaper editor, decides to write her own paper and Mr. Larson is her first subject. The biting editorial helps Mr. Larson become what he used to be: a good teacher! Clara discovers that truth and mercy can honestly tell a story, preserver the freedom of the press, and promote self-worth and dignity. (131 pages with full-page illustrations)

Title: *The Skin I'm In,* Sharon G. Flake (1998) (1999 Coretta Scott King Award, 1999 ALA Quick Pick for Reluctant Young Adult Readers, 1999 ALA Best Book for Young Adults). NY: Jump at the Sun, Hyperion Paperbacks for Children.

RL middle 3rd grade; **IL** 7th grade and up

Summary: Maleeka is 13 years old and has troubles. She is teased because of what she wears (her mother's handmade clothes that never fit or hold together), and she is very black. She is also friends with Charlese (Char), who loans her clothes in return for doing her homework. When Ms. Sanders becomes the new teacher, Maleeka finds a supporter who appreciates her writing talent as well as someone who has had to deal with differences. (Ms. Sanders has a skin condition that leaves one side of her face disfigured.) When Char convinces Maleeka to help her "pay back" Ms. Sanders for low grades, Maleeka, alone, is caught for vandalism and must come to terms with her own values and feelings. Maleeka's loving relationship with her mother remains a constant force as well as her friendship with Caleb, a classmate who likes Maleeka for her intelligence and her blackness. Flake's strong, believable characters and important theme reflect the conflict between wanting to fit in and being true to one's self. (171 pages)

Title: *What Do Fish Have to Do with Anything?,* Avi (1997). Cambridge, MA: Candlewick Press.

RL 3rd grade; **IL** 3rd–7th grade

Summary: This fascinating collection of short stories describes Willie, Matt Kaizer, Gregory, and others as they are involved in experiences that challenge their thinking and lead them to different points of view. For example, in *Teacher Tamer* (pp. 91–118), 5th grader Gregory discovers the true meaning behind his teacher's accusations of misbehavior. *Pets,* an unsettling ghost story about cats, is described under Ghosts. Each story is around 25 pages. (196 pages)

Title: *Wringer,* Jerry Spinelli (1997) (Newbery Honor Book). NY: Harper Trophy, a division of HarperCollins.

RL high 3rd to low 4th grade; **IL** 4th–7th grade

Summary: Palmer will soon be 10 and, unlike his friends, he dreads this birthday. Ten-year-olds in the rural town of Waymer become a "wringer," boys who wring the necks of pigeons that are wounded at the annual family fest—Pigeon Day. This is the day when thousands of pigeons (trapped or bought from local breeders) are released for participants to shoot, and the winner awarded the sharpshooter's trophy. When a pigeon lands on Palmer's windowsill, Palmer realizes that keeping the pigeon will only endanger the bird's life. The pigeon's friendship and loyalty to Palmer, which is reciprocated in-kind by the sensitive 10-year-old, creates a conflict that becomes deadly the day of the pigeon shoot. (228 pages)

IMMIGRANTS

PICTURE BOOKS

Title: *Going Home,* Eve Bunting, illustrated by David Diaz (1996). NY: Joanna Cotler Books, an imprint of HarperCollins.

RL 3rd grade; **IL** K–5th grade

Summary: Carlos, five-year-old sister Nora, and 10-year-old sister Dolores travel with their mother and father to Mexico to spend Christmas with their grandparents. Carlos' parents are legal farmworkers, leaving their beloved homeland to do backbreaking work in the strawberry fields in order to provide better opportunities for their children. When they reach La Perla, a small Mexican village, the happy family celebrates Christmas with grandparents, uncles, aunts, nieces, and nephews. The charming text and colorful, bold, whimsical illustrations celebrate the closeness of family and love of homeland. (30 pages)

Title: *Grandfather's Journey,* Allen Say (1993) (Caldecott Medal). Boston, MA: Houghton Mifflin.

RL low 4th grade; **IL** 1st–6th grade

Summary: The author/illustrator's gentle watercolors and eloquent story describe the journey his grandfather makes as a young man from Japan to San Francisco, California. There, he marries and raises a daughter before returning to Japan. In Japan his daughter marries and has a son. But the grandfather misses the mountains and rivers of California and plans a return visit. When the war breaks out, his plans are ended and he is never to return. The author's soft watercolors and realistic paintings poignantly illustrate this story of a love for two homelands. *Tree of Cranes* (about the author's first Christmas in Japan) and *Tea and Milk* (about his parents' courtship) also celebrate the beauty of two cultures. (32 pages)

Title: *I Have An Olive Tree,* Eve Bunting, illustrations by Karen Barbour (1999) (Picture Book). NY: Joanna Cotler Books, an imprint of HarperCollins.

RL 3rd grade; **IL** K–4th grade.

Summary: This inspiring, moving picture book tells the story of eight-year-old Sophia, who is given an olive tree from her grandfather for her birthday. The tree grows on a Greek island that was once home to her grandparents and mother. Before grandfather dies, he requests that Sophia and her mother travel to Greece and hang grandmother's necklace from a branch. Grandfather had carried the beads with him since the death of his wife. With money that grandfather had been saving over the years for this trip, Sophia and her mother find the knotted old tree and lovingly hang the beads from a branch. This makes a good read aloud story because of the longer sentences. (30 pages)

EASY READING/SHORT CHAPTER BOOKS

Title: *The Skirt,* Gary Soto (1992). NY: Bantam Doubleday Dell.

RL 4th grade; **IL** 3rd–6th grade

Summary: Miata's mother is from Mexico and is very proud of her folklorico skirt that she wore as a little girl. When Miata is given permission to take the skirt to school to show her friends before the Sunday folklorico dance, she mistakenly leaves the skirt on the school bus. Miata convinces her anxious friend, Ana, to help her slip into the bus parking lot and retrieve the skirt. But nothing is as easy as it looks! (74 pages)

NONFICTION

Title: *Roberto Clemente,* James Buckley, Jr. (2001). NY: Dorling Kindersley Readers.
RL 6th grade; **IL** all ages
Summary: See Sports.

FICTION

Title: *Baseball in April and Other Short Stories,* Gary Soto (1990) (ALA Best Book for Young Adults). NY: Harcourt.
RL middle 5th grade; **IL** 3rd–7th grade
Summary: See Identity/Solving Problems.

Title: *Esperanza Rising,* Pam Muñoz Ryan (2000). NY: Scholastic Press.
RL 5th grade; **IL** 5th–8th grade
Summary: See Identity/Solving Problems.

Title: *Seedfolks,* Paul Fleischman (1997), (ALA Best Books for Young Adults, ALA Quick Picks for Young Adults, IRA Children's Choices). NY: Harper Trophy, a division of HarperCollins.
RL high 3rd grade; **IL** 5th grade and up
Summary: Kim Young, a nine-year-old immigrant from Vietnam, plants beans in a nearby vacant lot that is filled with trash, rats, and ugliness. This small act inspires 13 other individuals that live in or around the apartment complex to do the same. The garden, soon filled with thriving vegetables and flowers, builds community, self-respect, and purpose, replacing the despair, loneliness, and neglect that once existed. The short chapters (three to four pages) richly present the diverse characters, old and young, that discover what a small plot of soil can accomplish. This is a heartwarming, inspiring story that celebrates diversity and the human spirit. (69 pages)

MYSTERY

EASY READING/SHORT CHAPTER BOOKS

Title: *Aunt Eater Loves A Mystery,* Dick King-Smith (1997). NY: Harper Trophy, a division of HarperCollins.
RL low 2nd grade; **IL** 1st–3rd grade
Summary: See Fantasy.

Title: *Cam Jansen and the Catnapping Mystery,* David Adler (1998). NY: Puffin Books.
RL 2nd grade; **IL** 2nd–5th grade
Summary: Cam (Jennifer) Jansen is called "Cam" because of her photogenic memory. When Cam says "Click," she calls up visual images to solve mysteries that no one else can remember! This time Cam, her friend Eric, and family are meeting her Aunt Molly at the Royal Hotel. As the family approaches the Royal, Cam notices a suspicious bellboy taking luggage and a cat from a hotel guest (Mrs. Wright) who later demands ransom money for their return. Cam comes to the aid of the police and a distraught Mrs. Wright when she describes in detail the get-a-way van and the bellboy's blue suit (the Royal Hotel has red suits!). This easy-to-read, entertaining mystery is one of a series. (58 pages)

Title: *Detective Dinosaur Lost and Found,* James Skofield (1998) (An I Can Read Book). NY: Harper Trophy, a division of Harper-Collins.
RL low 2nd grade; **IL** 1st–3rd grade
Summary: See Fantasy.

Title: *Encyclopedia Brown and the Case of the Mysterious Handprints,* Donald Sobol (1985). NY: Bantam Books.
RL 4th grade; **IL** 3rd–7th grade
Summary: Each chapter poses another mystery for Encyclopedia (LeRoy) Brown, son of Idaville police chief. Encyclopedia is named for his ability to read and remember everything that he can get his hands on. Unbeknownst to the town, Encyclopedia helps his dad with

mysteries that seem unsolveable. Each short chapter, telling a different story and ending without a solution, ends with a question and page number for the reader to find the answer (e.g., "Why? Turn to page 72 for the solution to 'The Case of the Blond Wig.'") (p. 9). (91 pages)

Title: *Encyclopedia Brown and the Case of the Slippery Salamander,* Donald Sobol (2000). NY: Bantom Skylark Books.
RL 4th grade; **IL** 3rd–7th grade
Summary: There are 10 short stories (each about seven pages long) with mysteries for the reader to solve. In the first story, *The Case of the Slippery Salamander,* Encyclopedia Brown helps his father solve the mystery of a missing tiger salamander, a valuable salamander that was recently acquired for the town's aquarium. A response from one of the three suspects gives Encyclopedia the evidence he needs. Can you guess why? The answer is on page 77! (87 pages)

Title: *Ghost Town at Sundown,* Mary Pope Osborne (1997) (Magic Tree House Series). NY: Random House.
RL 2nd grade; **IL** 1st–4th grade
Summary: Jack and Annie receive instructions from enchantress librarian Morgan le Fay to solve three riddles in the time of the wild, wild west. Whisked away in the magic tree house to Rattlesnake Flats, a deserted western prairie town, the children encounter horse thieves; wild mustangs; a mustang herder named Slim; and Lonesome Luke, a melancholy cowboy ghost who wanders the prairie looking for his lost sweetheart. This is a short chapter book with surprises! (73 pages)

Title: *In a Dark, Dark Room and Other Scary Stories,* retold by Alvin Schwartz (1984). NY: HarperCollins.
RL low 1st grade; **IL** 1st–4th grade
Summary: See Ghosts.

Title: *Nate the Great and the Monster Mess,* Marjorie Seinman Sharmat (1999). NY: Delacorte Press, a division of Random House.
RL 1st grade; **IL** 1st–3rd grade
Summary: Nate and his dog Sludge are trying to find his mother's lost recipe for Monster Cookies. Questioning neighbors and supermar-

ket clerks and sorting through old recipes prove fruitless. Will Nate un-
cover this mystery? Vivid watercolors and large print make these stories easy to read and enjoyable. There are many other clever stories
from the Nate the Great series. (48 pages)

Title: *Spider Kane and the Mystery at Jumbo Nightcrawler's,* Mary
Pope Osborne (1999) (Stepping Stone edition). NY: Random House.

RL 4th grade; **IL** 3rd–5th grade

Summary: Four friends and comrades in the Order of the Moth receive a note from Spider Kane, leader of the Order, to meet at Jumbo
Nightcrawler's Supper Club on Waterfront Row. All mysteriously dis-
appear! Leon Leafwing—a good friend of Mimi and the gossamer-
winged butterfly who is one of the victims—discovers that Spider Kane
did not write the note. It is up to Spider and Leon to solve the mystery,
find Leon's mother, and rescue their friends before Bald Buzzer (alias
Raymond Johnson) carries out his threats with his hornet gang in his
search for gold. A fun story with wild names and characters (Little
Pickles, Thomas "The Hawk" Hawkins, La Mere Leafwing, Walter
Dogtick, Saratoga D'Bee) and exciting story events! (124 pages)

Title: *The High-Rise Private Eyes: The Case of the Puzzling Possum,* Cynthia Rylant (2001). Hong Kong, S. China Printing Co.: Greenwillow Books, HarperCollins.

RL 2nd grade; **IL** 1st–4th grade

Summary: See Fantasy.

Title: *The Lucky Lottery, A to Z Mysteries,* Ron Roy (2000) (Stepping Stone edition). NY: Random House.

RL 2nd grade; **IL** 1st–4th grade

Summary: Who has stolen a winning lottery ticket worth seven mil-
lion dollars? Dink, Ruth Ann, and Josh must find the thief because the
missing ticket belongs to their friend, Lucky. Lucky's grandfather had
enclosed it in a Christmas card to his grandson. First the children find
footprints, small tinfoil bow ties, and a few suspicious characters that
live with Lucky's grandfather in a home for the elderly. Dot Calm, a
friendly young woman who sells lottery tickets, provides clues that
lead the three detectives away from the culprit. (87 pages)

Title: *The Missing Mummy, A to Z Mysteries,* Ron Roy (2001) (Stepping Stone edition). NY: Random House.

RL 2nd grade; **IL** 1st–4th grade

Summary: Dink, Josh, and Ruth Rose visit the Wadsworth Museum for Mummy Monday Day and find themselves in a middle of a baffling mystery: Who snatched and then returned a child mummy? What was hidden inside the mummy's tomb? What does museum director Dr. Tweed have to do with it all? Clues include short dark hair, gravel, and the smell of french fries! Again the young detectives trace a series of clues to find the culprits. (83 pages)

Title: *The Panther Mystery: The Boxcar Children,* created by Gertrude Chandler Warner (1998). NY: Albert Whitman & Company.

RL 3rd grade; **IL** 2nd–7th grade

Summary: The four resourceful and independent orphan children, Henry, Jessie, Violet, and Benny (ranging in age from six to 14), live with their grandfather. The title of the series describes the home (i.e., boxcar) that the children first lived in after the death of their parents. In this story, number 66 in the series, the children and grandfather attempt to rescue a missing ranger in the Everglades who is tracking a valuable panther and a suspected poacher. (123 pages)

FICTION

Title: *Bunnicula: A Rabbit-Tale of Mystery,* Deborah and James Howe (1979). NY: Avon Books.

RL 3rd grade; **IL** 3rd–7th grade

Summary: See Humor.

Title: *Bunnicula Strikes Again!,* James Howe (1999). NY: Atheneum Books, an imprint of Simon & Schuster Children's Publishing Division.

RL middle 4th grade; **IL** 3rd–7th grade

Summary: See Humor.

Title: *Coffin on a Case,* Eve Bunting (1992) (Egar Winner, Mystery Writers of America). NY: HarperTrophy.

RL 3rd grade; **IL** 4th–8th grade

Summary: Sixth grader Henry Coffin helps his detective father and partner, George Pale, solve cases for the Coffin and Pale Detective Agency. Henry has two fantasies: (1) that a beautiful "babe" will walk in the door with a case to solve; and (2) that his mother, who left home when he was six weeks old to pursue a more glamorous life, will walk in the door and make the family complete again. The first fantasy comes true when pretty, distressed, 16-year-old Lily Larson seeks help from his father to find her mother who did not return home from selling wooden storks to new parents. Henry's dad, who doubts that Mrs. Larson is really missing and is ready to leave for San Diego to help his partner complete an investigation, advises the worried teenager to go to the police. A stubborn Lily returns and convinces Henry to take the case. Bunting's book is a fast-paced page- turner written in first person from Henry's point of view. Both Henry and his father are fans of the old time fictional character, detective Sam Spade ("The Maltese Falcon"). The mystery is full of clipped dialogue (in Sam Spade style), an exciting plot (museum thieves, a mother trapped in a deserted basement, a murky pond that provides a hiding place for Henry and the Divine Scholar) and believable characters. (105 pages).

Title: *Dead Letter: A Herculeah Jones Mystery,* Betsy Byars (1996) (IRA Children's Choices). NY: Puffin Books, Penguin Group.
RL 3rd grade; **IL** 4th–7th grade
Summary: Herculeah is drawn to a coat inside a secondhand store. It seems to be made for her, but when she tries it on her hair begins to frizzle (always a sign of danger) and the mystery begins. To whom does the letter belong inside of the lining? Is horsewoman Amanda Cole murdered rather than accidentally killed? And will Meat, Herculeah's friend, find her in time to prevent another murder? There is lots of suspense in this easy-to-read, fast-paced mystery story. Don't miss *Disappearing Acts,* another Herculeah Jones Mystery. (147 pages)

Title: *Dew Drop Dead,* James Howe (1990) (A Sebastian Barth Mystery). NY: Aladdin Paperbacks.
RL middle 4th grade, **IL** 3rd–8th grade
Summary: Twelve-year-old Sebastian and his friends, David and Corrie, bicycle to the deserted Dew Drop Inn, climb in an open win-

dow, and see a body draped over the bed in an upstairs bedroom! When they report the "murder" to dubious detective chief Alex Theopoulos and deputy Rebecca Quinn, the five return to the old Inn to find that the body is missing. When the three young investigators find the lifeless body next to a blood-spattered rock in the nearby woods, the search for the murderer begins. Corrie's father, a minister, shelters homeless people in his church and one suspect is "Abraham," a homeless man whom Corrie befriends while helping her father with the shelter. The author weaves in social concerns, family upsets, and a suspenseful plot with clues that point to the innocent mentally ill Abraham. In the end the murder is solved, Abraham's identity is revealed, and the Dew Drop Inn becomes a shelter for the homeless. (short chapters, 156 pages)

Title: *Holes,* Louis Sachar (1998) (National Book Award, Newbery Award, ALA Quick Pick for Reluctant Readers). NY: Frances Foster Books, Farrar, Straus and Giroux.
RL high 3rd grade; **IL** 4th grade and up
Summary: See Adventure/Survival.

Title: *Midnight Magic,* Avi (1999) (ALA Quick Picks for Reluctant Young Adult Readers). NY: Scholastic Press.
RL low 5th grade; **IL** 4th–9th grade
Summary: See Ghosts.

Title: *Something Upstairs,* Avi (1997). NY: Avon Books.
RL middle 4th grade; **IL** 3rd–7th grade
Summary: Kenny Huldorf and his parents have just moved to Providence, Rhode Island, into the Daniel Stillwell House, built in 1789. Sleeping on the top floor, Kenny hears a scratching sound and discovers Caleb (a ghost) frantically trying to escape the four enclosed walls. Caleb, Stillwell's young slave who was shot in the back in the locked attic, persuades Kenny to travel back in time to find his murderer. Avi builds his suspenseful story on events that occurred in Providence in the early 1800s. (199 pages)

Title: *Who Stole the Wizard of Oz?,* Avi (1981). NY: Alfred Knopf.
RL 3rd grade; **IL** 3rd–7th grade
Summary: It is summer vacation and Becky decides to begin her

summer reports. When she goes to the library to find *The Wizard of Oz,* she is told to come back tomorrow because the book will be on sale. Returning the next day, Becky is surprised to discover that the book has been stolen and that she is the suspect! (117 pages)

Title: *The Case of the Lion Dance,* Lawrence Yep (1998). NY: HarperTrophy.
RL low 4th grade; **IL** 3rd–7th grade
Summary: Lily watches horrified as a bomb explodes a ball of $2,000 bills during the festive Lion Dance, hurting her friend Barry, a kung fu dancer in the lion costume. It is up to Lily and her famous Auntie Lil to find the thief. Rival kung fu performers, feuding relatives, a mysterious carnation pot, and threatening notes are part of this exciting mystery set in San Francisco's Chinatown. (214 pages)

NONFICTION

PICTURE BOOKS

Title: *A Blue Butterfly, A Story About Claude Monet,* Bijou Le Tord (1995). NY: Delacorte Press, Bantam Doubleday Dell.
RL not applicable; **IL** 1st–6th grade
Summary: See Art.

Title: *A Day in the Life of a Dancer,* Linda Hayward (2001) (Dorling Kindersley Readers, level 1). NY: Dorling Kindersley.
RL 1st grade; **IL** all ages
Summary: Colorful action photographs and large-print, easy vocabulary, describe a day in the life of dancer Lisa Torres. From packing her bag to going to the ballet company at 9:00 a.m. to talking to her roommate at 11:00 p.m. about her thrilling performance, Lisa allows the reader to share her exciting day as a ballerina. A picture word list of dancing terms follow the easy text. (32 pages)

Title: *Diego,* Jeanette Winter (1991). NY: Alfred A. Knopf.
RL low 3rd grade; **IL** 1st–6th grade
Summary: See Art.

Title: *Francisco Goya,* Mike Venezia (1991). Chicago, IL: Children's Press.
RL 5th grade; **IL** 3rd–6th grade
Summary: See Art.

Title: *I Dreamed I Was a Ballerina,* a girlhood story by Anna Pavlova, illustrated with art by Degas Degas (2001). NY: Metropolitan Museum of Art, Atheneum Books for Young Readers.
RL 6th grade; **IL** all ages
Summary: See Dance.

Title: *Leonardo's Horse,* Jean Fritz (2001). NY: G. P. Putnam's Sons.
RL 6th grade; **IL** all ages
Summary: See Art.

Title: *Martin's Big Words: The Life of Dr. Martin Luther King, Jr.,* Doreen Rappaport (2001). NY: Hyperion Books.
RL 4th grade; **IL** all ages
Summary: See Biography.

Title: *My Secret Camera: Life in the Lodz Ghetto,* photographs by Mendel Grossman, text by Frank Dabba Smith (2000). NY: Gulliver Books, Harcourt.
RL high 3rd grade; **IL** 4th grade and up
Summary: Simple text and moving black-and-white photographs describe the bravery, hardship, and community of Jewish individuals imprisoned in the Lodz Ghetto in Poland. (32 pages)

Title: *Paul Gauguin,* Mike Venezia (1993). Chicago, IL: Children's Press.
RL 5th grade; **IL** 3rd–6th grade
Summary: See Art.

Title: *Red-Eyed Tree Frog,* by Joy Cowley, photographs by Nic Bishop (1999). NY: Scholastic.
RL not applicable; **IL** 1st–5th grade

Summary: Twenty-six short sentences and colorful action photographs of the red-eyed tree frog that live in the rain forests of Central America will entrance wildlife enthusiasts. Readers will see close up photographs of the frog leaping, flicking its tongue, hopping, eating, and experiencing other activities during a day in the rain forest. (30 pages)

Title: *Shooting for the Moon: The Amazing Life and Times of Annie Oakley,* Stephen Krensky (2001). NY: Melanie Kroupa Books, Farrar, Straus and Giroux.
RL 3rd grade; **IL** all ages
Summary: See Biography.

Title: *The Dinosaurs of Waterhouse Hawkins,* Barbara Kerley (2001). NY: Scholastic Press.
RL 5th grade; **IL** all ages
Summary: See Art.

EASY READING/SHORT CHAPTER BOOKS

Title: *Dinosaurs, Magic Tree House Research Guide,* Will Osborne and Mary Pope Osborne (2000). NY: Random House.
RL 2nd grade; **IL** 1st–4th grade
Summary: This nonfiction companion to the author's mystery *Dinosaurs Before Dark,* is a fascinating book for anyone that is interested in knowing more about dinosaurs. Divided into eight short chapters, the authors describe the Mesozoic Era of reptiles (Triassic, Jurassic, and Cretaceous Periods), dinosaur names and characteristics (e.g., flesh-eaters and plant-eaters), theories on the end of the dinosaur period, and end with more questions and mysteries for avid readers. Black-and-white illustrations are interspersed with informative text. Research information and a good index follow the text. (119 pages with index)

Title: *Free at Last! The Story of Martin Luther King, Jr.,* Angela Bull (2000). NY: Dorling Kindersley Readers.
RL 6th grade; **IL** all ages
Summary: Six short chapters describe the dramatic life of Martin

Luther King, Jr. From being baptized in his father's church at age five to his tragic death in 1968 in Memphis, this short chapter book illustrates the accomplishments of this great man who was to become the youngest recipient of the Nobel Peace Prize. Sidebars and black-and-white and color photographs depict important events in the Civil Rights Movements such as Rosa Parks' refusal to give up her bus seat, sit-ins at white-only lunch counters, the Freedom Riders, Martin's march from Selma to Montgomery, and his famous speech at the Lincoln Memorial on August 28, 1963. (49 pages including the index)

Title: *Mummies and Pyramids, Magic Tree House Research Guide,* Will Osborne and Mary Pope Osborne (2001). NY: Random House.
RL 2nd grade; **IL** 1st–4th grade
Summary: This nonfiction companion to *Mummies in the Morning* is a great resource on mummies. The nine short chapters include facts and accompanying illustrations on ancient Egypt, the people (religion, work, family life, homes, hieroglyphic writing, funerals), mummies (why and how they were constructed), and the loss of treasured artifacts by tomb robbers. Readers will discover the wonders of King Tutankhamun's tomb; read about the Egyptologist who made this important discovery; and find a list of resources that include books, museums, Web sites, and CD-ROMs. (199 pages with index)

Title: *NFL's Greatest Upsets,* James Buckley, Jr. (2000). NY: Dorling Kindersley Readers.
RL 6th grade; **IL** all ages
Summary: See Sports.

Title: *Roberto Clemente,* James Buckley, Jr. (2001). NY: Dorling Kindersley Readers.
RL 6th grade; **IL** all ages
Summary: See Sports.

Title: *Strikeout Kings,* James Buckley, Jr. (2001). NY: Dorling Kindersley Readers.
RL high 3rd to low 4th grade; **IL** all ages
Summary: See Sports.

POETRY

Title: *Insect Soup: Bug Poems,* Barry Louis Polisar (1999). Silver Spring, MD: Rainbow Morning Music.
RL not applicable; **IL** 1st–5th grade
Summary: See Poetry.

POETRY AND RHYMING TEXT

Title: *A Light in the Attic,* Shel Silverstein (1981). NY: Harper & Row Publishers.
RL not applicable; **IL** all ages
Summary: Hilarious, quirky poems that are easy to read are accompanied by the poet's whimsical, funny pen-and-ink illustrations. Some poems consist of only a few sentences while others are longer narratives. Be sure to read Shel Sivlerstein's other delightful poetry collections entitled, *Where the Sidewalk Ends* (1974) and *Falling Up* (1996). (169 pages)

Title: *A Pizza the Size of the Sun,* Jack Prelutsky (1994, 1996) (ALA Notable Book). NY: Greenwillow Books.
RL not applicable; **IL** 1st–7th grade
Summary: A funny collection of poems (some only four lines, other longer) that are accompanied by humorous pen-and-ink drawings. You'll read about Mister Pfister Gristletwist, An Unobservant Porcupine, Rat for Lunch, and read what it feels like to be All Mixed Up! (153 pages)

Title: *Brown Angels,* Walter Dean Myers (1993) (Picture Book). NY: HarperCollins.
RL not applicable; **IL** all ages
Summary: Forty-two turn-of-the-century photographs and 11 joyous poems celebrate the children whose photographs grace these pages. The photographs are from the poet's collection. His verses describe a range of feelings and experiences that compliment each photograph, such as Jeannie Had a Giggle, Pride, Friendship, Pretty Little Black Girl, and Summer. (33 pages)

Title: *Casey at the Bat: A Ballad of the Republic Sung in the Year 1888,* Christopher Bing (2000) (Caldecott Honor Book). NY: Handprint Books.

RL not applicable; **IL** all ages

Summary: This amazing picture book illustrates the classic poem (ballad) by E. L. Thayer, *Casey at the Bat,* published in the 1888 issue of the *San Francisco Examiner.* Along with a line or two of verse and full-page black-and-white illustrations mirroring the engraving technique of the late 19th century, Bing includes reproductions of old baseball cards, tickets, advertisements, money, and snippets from the *1888 National Sports Report & Gazette.* This is a fascinating, read aloud picture book that brings the Mighty Casey and Mudville fans alive, springing from the pages. If you haven't read about Casey striking out, now is the time to do it! (32 pages)

Title: *Everett Anderson's Goodbye,* by Lucille Clifton, illustrated by Ann Grifalconi (1983) (Coretta Scott King Award). NY: Henry Holt, and Company.

RL not applicable; **IL** all ages

Summary: In moving verse and soft charcoal illustrations, the poet gently expresses the five stages of grief as Everett Anderson learns to say goodbye to his father. (28 pages)

Title: *Extra Innings: Baseball Poems,* selected by Lee Bennett Hopkins (1993). NY: Harcourt Brace & Company.

RL not applicable; **IL** 3rd–7th grade

Summary: Short and longer narratives tell about the glory of watching and playing baseball. Readers will find Joe DiMaggio and the Mighty Casey (from Mudville) in the collection. Bright watercolor illustrations by Scott Medlock capture the energy in the rhyming and free verse. (39 pages)

Title: *Falling Up,* Shel Silverstein (1996). NY: HarperCollins.

RL not applicable; **IL** all ages

Summary: Witty poems and drawings depict such characters as Reachin' Richard, Web-Foot Woe, Weird-Bird, and Screamin' Millie. All of these hilarious poems rhyme and are great fun to hear and read! (171 pages)

Title: *Flower Garden,* Eve Bunting (1994) (A Parenting Outstanding Book of the Year). NY: Voyager Books, Harcourt.
RL not applicable; **IL** K–3rd grade
Summary: See Family Relationships.

Title: *For Laughing Out Loud: Poems to Tickle Your Funnybone,* Jack Prelutsky (1991). NY: Alfred A. Knopf.
RL not applicable; **IL** 1st–6th grade
Summary: Short, funny poems by well-known poets make up this wonderful collection. Vivid, splashy watercolors illustrate each poem. Many poems are only four lines and are fun to read and reread. (78 pages)

Title: *Green Eggs and Ham,* Dr. Seuss (1960). NY: Random House.
RL 1st grade; **IL** K–4th grade
Summary: See Humor.

Title: *If Pigs Could Fly . . . And Other Deep Thoughts,* Bruce Lansky (2000). NY: Meadowbrook Press, distributed by Simon & Schuster.
RL not applicable; **IL** 1st–6th grade
Summary: A collection of humorous poems that describe experiences that children can relate to and laugh about. Examples of the nine categories include Parents and Other Geezers, School Days, Love and Other Diseases, My Twisted Imagination, and What I've Learned About Life. Some poems have only one stanza while others have seven or eight. All are funny, rhyme, and easy to read. (81 pages)

Title: *Insect Soup: Bug Poems,* Barry Louis Polisar (1999). Silver Spring, MD: Rainbow Morning Music.
RL not applicable; **IL** 1st–5th grade
Summary: The three-time Parent's Choice Award winner writes humorous, short poems about all kinds of insects that include the Saddleback Caterpillar, House Fly, Flea, Butterfly, and Chiggers. David Clarks' comic style watercolor illustrations add to the fun of this picture book collection. (30 pages)

Title: *No More Homework! No More Tests! Kids' Favorite Funny School Poems,* selected by Bruce Lansky (1997). NY: Meadowbrook Press, Simon & Schuster.

RL not applicable; **IL** 1st–6th grade

Summary: This funny poetry book is all about school. Bruce Lansky collects poems by well-known poets like Shel Silverstein and Jack Prelutsky. Cartoon drawings accompany the humorous poems that children will love to relate to. Many are short, and all are good for reading and rereading. (71 pages)

Title: *Love That Dog,* Sharon Creech (2001). NY: Joanna Cotler Books, HarperCollins.

RL 2nd grade; **IL** 3rd–7th grade

Summary: See Humor.

Title: *My Many Colored Days,* Dr. Seuss (1996). NY: Alfred A. Knopf.

RL not applicable; **IL** all ages

Summary: Color words and rhyming verse depict feelings and moods in Dr. Seuss' expressive book written in 1973 and published in 1996 with the colorful, splashy paintings of Steve Johnson and Lou Fancher. Color days such as yellow, blue, red, orange, and black depict feelings that all have experienced! (28 pages)

Title: *Oh, the Places You'll Go!,* Dr. Seuss (1990). NY: Random House.

RL 1st grade; **IL** 3rd grade and up

Summary: See Identity/Solving Problems.

Title: *Quiet Storm: Voices of Young Black Poets,* selected by Lydia Omolola Okutoro (1999, 2000 ALA Quick Picks for Reluctant Young Adult Readers). NY: Jump at the Sun, Hyperion Books for Children.

RL not applicable; **IL** all ages

Summary: The 61 poems in this collection are written by young black poets (ages 13–21) from Canada, England, and the United States. Poets are from Jamaica, Haiti, Barbados, Panama, Nigeria, Somalia, St.

Thomas, Zaire, and Uganda. The collection is grouped according to categories such as Black Pride, Unity, Beauty, Hopes and Dreams of a Brighter Future, and the Poet as Keeper of the Oral Tradition. Simple words that eloquently express thoughts, feelings, and ideas inspire readers. (84 pages)

Title: *Salting the Ocean: 100 Poems by Young Poets,* selected by Naomi Shihab Nye (2000). NY: Greenwillow Books, an imprint of HarperCollins.

RL not applicable; **IL** 1st–12th grade

Summary: The author has collected 100 poems written by individuals when they were children in 1st–12th grade. As Nye notes, the poets represent professions that include dancers, teachers, dentists, students, and construction workers. The inspiring poems tell about everyday experiences such as First Love (p. 70), Winter (p. 43), Monday Mornings (p. 15), and How to Grow Up (pp. 8–9). As the collector notes, we all can be poets! (105 pages)

Title: *Sports! Sports! Sports! A Poetry Collection,* selected by Lee Bennett Hopkins (1999) (An I Can Read Book). NY: HarperCollins.

RL not applicable; **IL** 1st–5th grade

Summary: These short poems, written in large, bold-faced type, describe the excitement and fun of playing sports. Baseball, basketball, football, ice hockey, soccer, skating, swimming, and running are all included! Exciting watercolors splash over each page and capture the energy in this small, readable collection. (47 pages)

Title: *The Basket Counts,* Arnold Adoff (2000). NY: Simon & Schuster Books for Young Readers.

RL not applicable; **IL** 3rd grade and up

Summary: Free verse poems accompanied by colorful, energetic illustrations describe the joy, frustration, and exuberant feelings when playing basketball. The distinguished poet creates type and space that illustrate words and add meaning to his work. Basketball players and enthusiasts particularly enjoy this small book of wonderful poetry. (46 pages)

Title: *The Cat in the Hat,* Dr. Seuss (1957).
RL 1st grade; **IL** K–3rd grade
Summary: See Humor.

Title: *Where the Sidewalk Ends,* Shel Silverstein (1974). NY: Harper & Row.
RL not applicable; **IL** all ages
Summary: This wonderful collection precedes *A Light in the Attic* and *Falling Up.* Like the other two books, whimsical line drawings illustrate the delightful and sometimes serious verse. This volume contains such favorites as *Sarah Cynthia Sylvia Stout Would Not Take the Garbage Out, Sick, Smart,* and *Band-Aids.* (166 pages)

ROMANCE

PICTURE BOOKS

Title: *Shooting for the Moon: The Amazing Life and Times of Annie Oakley,* Stephen Krensky (2001). NY: Melanie Kroupa Books, Farrar, Straus and Giroux.
RL 3rd grade; **IL** all ages
Summary: See Biography.

Title: *Tea with Milk,* Allen Say (1999). Boston: Houghton Mifflin.
RL high 4th grade; **IL** 2nd–6th grade
Summary: Elegant watercolor illustrations depict the young life and courtship of Masako (May), the author's mother, who grows up in San Francisco and returns as a young woman to Japan, her parents' homeland. Working in Osako, May meets a young man whom she will later marry. While sipping tea with milk, May and Joseph talk about making a home together, a place that encompasses both cultures. (32 pages)

EASY READING/SHORT CHAPTER BOOKS

Title: *In Aunt Lucy's Kitchen—The Cobble Street Cousins,* Cynthia Rylant (1998). NY: Aladdin Paperpacks.
RL middle 2nd grade; **IL** 2nd–5th grade
Summary: See Family Relationships.

Title: *Sarah, Plain and Tall,* Patricia MacLachlan (1985) (Newbery Medal). NY: Harper Trophy, a division of HarperCollins.
RL 3rd grade; **IL** 3rd–7th grade
Summary: See Historical Fiction.

Title: *Summer Party—The Cobble Street Cousins,* by Cynthia Rylant (2001). NY: Simon & Schuster Books for Young Readers, an imprint of Simon & Schuster Children's Publishing Division.
RL middle 2nd grade; **IL** 2nd–5th grade
Summary: See Family Relationships.

Title: *The King's Equal,* Katherine Paterson (1992) (Trophy Chapter Book). NY: Harper Trophy, a division of HarperCollins.
RL 3rd grade; **IL** 2nd–5th grade
Summary: See Fantasy.

FICTION

Title: *Beauty Lessons* from *An Island Like You: Stories of the Barrio* (pp. 41–54), Judith Ortiz Cofer (1995). (ALA Best Book for Young Adults, Pura Belpre Award). NY: Puffin Books.
RL 5th grade; **IL** 7th–12th grade
Summary: Sandra knows that Paco, one of the best students in Mrs. Laguna's algebra class, is looking at her. But Sandra is not popular or good-looking. Rather, she is a late-bloomer, says her teacher, "and flowers that bloom slowly last longer" (p. 47). Sandra decides to take beauty lessons from her aunt Modesta, a striking woman who knows how to wear makeup, until she realizes that Modesta's beauty is false (false eyelashes, contact lenses, makeup) and that Paco appreciates Sandra for her true self. (13 pages)

Title: *Broken Chain* from *Baseball in April and Other Short Stories* (pp. 1–12), Gary Soto (1990). NY: Harcourt.
RL middle 5th grade; **IL** 3rd–7th grade
Summary: Alfonso wants to take his new girlfriend Sandra on a bike ride but needs two bikes! Sandra's bike has a flat tire, and his bike has a broken chain. His brother has already said no to loaning Alfonso his bike because of a fishing trip. What can he do? He has promised

Sandra that he would meet her with an extra bike! (This is the first story in a collection of short stories.)

Title: *Esperanza Rising,* Pam Muñoz Ryan (2000). NY: Scholastic Press.
RL 5th grade; **IL** 5th–8th grade
Summary: See Identity/Solving Problems.

Title: *Ella Enchanted,* Gail Carson Levin (1997) (Newbery Honor). NY: Harper Trophy, a division of HarperCollins.
RL 3rd grade; **IL** 3rd–10th grade
Summary: See Fantasy.

Title: *Just Ella,* Margaret Peterson Haddix (1999). NY: Simon and Schuster.
RL low 5th grade; **IL** 6th grade and up
Summary: See Fantasy.

SPORTS

PICTURE BOOKS

Title: *Hoops with Swoopes,* Susan Kuklin with Sheryl Swoopes (2001). NY: Jump at the Sun, Hyperion Books for Children.
RL not applicable; **IL** 1st–3rd grade
Summary: Large print, 13 sentences, and 94 words accompany full-page color photographs of Sheryl Swoopes, a member of the Houston Comets (the WNBA champions from 1997–2000), who was recently named the WNBA Most Valuable Player of the Year. This is a colorful, easy-to-read picture book with action-packed pictures of the talented basketball player. (30 pages)

EASY READING/SHORT CHAPTER BOOKS

Title: *I Can't Accept Not Trying: Michael Jordan on the Pursuit of Excellence,* Michael Jordan (1994). NY: HarperCollins.
RL 4th grade; **IL** 4th–9th grade

Summary: This inspiring little book of six chapters and 36 pages describes Michael Jordan's philosophy about life that includes setting goals, practicing, taking small steps, and not being afraid of failing. These are a few of the important principles that the reader will discover. Each chapter contains black-and-white photographs of the famous athlete. (36 pages)

Title: *NFL's Greatest Upsets,* James Buckley, Jr. (2000). NY: Dorling Kindersley Readers.

RL 6th grade; **IL** all ages

Summary: Action photographs and informative text describe the historic upsets that have taken place in the National Football League. Hall of Fame recipients include Joe Namath; Colts kicker Lou Michaels; Cowboys quarterback Roger Staubach; and Jacksonville's defensive end, Clyde Simmons along with other famous players that have changed football history. Sidebars with photographs provide additional information. (48 pages with glossary)

Title: *Roberto Clemente,* James Buckley, Jr. (2001). NY: Dorling Kindersley Readers.

RL 6th grade; **IL** all ages

Summary: Roberto Clemente, the son of parents who worked on a sugarcane farm in Puerto Rico, became one of the best hitters of all times and one of the greatest right fielders in baseball history. This short five-chapter book is filled with photographs and readable, large-print text that describe and salute the life of this great athlete. Playing baseball in Puerto Rico, young Roberto used a bat made from a guava tree and a glove from an old coffee sack. He was to become a hero to baseball and to the Puerto Rican community, yet he suffered discrimination in the United States as a person of color. The informative text is filled with color and black-and-white photographs with sidebars that provide additional facts. The author describes the rich contributions that Roberto Clemente made to baseball and to the children of Puerto Rico. (49 pages including index and glossary)

Title: *Strikeout Kings,* James Buckley, Jr. (2001). NY: Dorling Kindersley Readers.

RL high 3rd to low 4th grade; **IL** all ages

Summary: This fascinating short chapter book describes the greatest pitchers of Major League Baseball during the past 100 years. Stars include Tim Keefe, who like others of that period didn't use a glove (NY Giants, 1880s); Christy Mathewson, master of the screwball (NY Giants, 1905); left-handed pitcher Sandy Koufax, who won five ERA titles (1962–1966); and Latin American pitcher Pedro Martinez with 305 strikeouts (1997). The reader will find large-print, fascinating text; sidebars with facts about baseball and pitchers; color and black-and-white action photographs; and familiar baseball vocabulary. (49 pages including index and glossary)

POETRY

Title: *Extra Innings: Baseball Poems,* selected by Lee Bennett Hopkins (1993). NY: Harcourt Brace & Company.
RL not applicable; **IL** 3rd–7th grade
Summary: See Poetry.

Title: *Sports! Sports! Sports! A Poetry Collection,* selected by Lee Bennett Hopkins (1999). NY: HarperCollins.
RL not applicable; **IL** 1st–5th grade
Summary: See Poetry.

Title: *The Basket Counts,* Arnold Adoff (2000). NY: Simon & Schuster.
RL not applicable; **IL** 3rd grade and up
Summary: See Poetry.

FICTION

Title: *Baseball in April* from *Baseball in April and Other Short Stories,* Gary Soto (1990). NY: Harcourt.
RL middle 5th grade; **IL** 3rd–7th grade
Summary: Michael and younger brother Jessie are trying out for the Little League Team for the third time in a row. Both brothers hope to

make the team this time, but will they? New opportunities surface when the boys fail to make the team. (A story in a collection of realistic short stories by Mexican American writer Gary Soto.) (pages 13–22)

Title: *Run, Billy, Run,* Matt Christopher (1980). Boston: Little Brown and Company.

RL middle 3rd grade; **IL** 5th–10th grade

Summary: Fourteen-year-old Billy Chekko lives in a small stucco home beyond the stone quarry and runs several miles most days on errands for his family. His father cannot afford a car; and Billy must run to town to get groceries, medicine for his ill sister (Christine), and locate the family doctor when she shows no improvement. When taunted about his running by Cody Jones, a 17-year-old bully, Billy decides to join the high school track team. Billy thinks he can run and wants to prove it, but things don't go his way. Billy misses practice to help his father chop wood, lets his studies slide, and makes a bet with Cody that damages his growing relationship with Wendy Thaler. With the support of his family, a tough but fair track coach, and Billy's own hard work and perseverance, Billy brings recognition to the town and school as he wins the two-mile race against Hamlin. (164 pages)

Title: *Slam,* Walter Dean Myers (1996) (Coretta Scott King Award). NY: Scholastic Press.

RL middle to high 4th grade; **IL** 5th grade and up

Summary: See Identity/Solving Problems.

Title: *Snowboard Maverick,* Matt Christopher (1997). NY: Little Brown & Company.

RL 4th grade; **IL** 5th–9th grade

Summary: Thirteen–year-old Dennis O'Malley is the best skateboarder in Moorsville. A prior skiing accident has frightened him of snowboarding when his friends try to persuade him to join them. After finally getting on a snowboard, Dennis realizes that this is the sport for him. When his parents surprise him with a snowboard for Christmas, Dennis goes out to the slopes with his friends and discovers that he has much to learn about snowboarding! When he is goaded into taking a bet racing against a seasoned skateboarder on a dangerous hill filled with trees, Dennis realizes that he has made a mistake that he will regret. (152 pages)

Title: *Taking Sides,* Gary Soto (1991). NY: Harcourt Brace & Company.
RL high 4th grade; **IL** 6th–10th grade
Summary: See Identity/Self-Esteem.

CHAPTER 5

Finding Resources

There are many resources that help guide parents and caretakers in selecting and using quality children's literature. This section provides book titles described in chapter 4 that are currently available on audiocassettes, videotapes, and in Spanish. Book clubs, children's magazines, Web sites, professional books, and organizations pertaining to literacy and children with learning difficulties are also listed.

BOOKS ON AUDIOTAPE

Listening to audiocassettes enables struggling readers to hear a book that may initially be too difficult to read and helps reinforce a book that they are currently reading or may want to read. Listening to professional readers provides a model for reading and develops listening comprehension skills. Word recognition is reinforced when readers follow along in books that accompany audiotapes. The following books on tape are described in chapter 4 and include fantasy, realistic fiction, historical fiction, and humorous stories.

- *A Long Way From Chicago,* Richard Peck, Listening Library
- *A Series of Unfortunate Events,* Lemony Snicket, Listening Library
- *A Year Down Yonder,* Richard Peck, Listening Library
- *Brian's Winter,* Gary Paulsen, Bantam Books
- *Bunnicula: A Rabbit-Tale of Mystery,* Deborah and James Howe, Listening Library
- *Bunnicula Strikes Again!,* James Howe, Listening Library

- *Ella Enchanted,* Gail Carson Levin, Bantam Books-Audio (also available in Thorndike Large Print edition)
- *Hachet,* Gary Paulsen, Bantam Doubleday Dell
- *Harry Potter and the Chamber of Secrets* (Book 2), J. K. Rowling, Listening Library
- *Harry Potter and the Goblet of Fire* (Book 4), J. K. Rowling, Listening Library
- *Harry Potter and the Prisoner of Azkaban* (Book 3), J. K. Rowling, Listening Library
- *Harry Potter and the Sorcerer's Stone* (Book 1), J. K. Rowling, Listening Library
- *Holes,* Louis Sachar, Listening Library
- *James and the Giant Peach,* Bolby Laboratories Listening Cooperation
- *Joey Pigza Loses Control,* Jack Gantos, Listening Library
- *Owl at Home,* Arnold Lobel, Harper Audio
- *Sarah Plain and Tall,* Patricia MacLahan, Harper Children's Audio
- *Sideway Stories from the Wayside School,* Louis Sachar, Listening Library
- *Superfudge,* Judy Plume, Listening Library
- *The Laundry News,* Listening Library
- *The Magic Tree House Collection,* Mary Pope Osborne, Listening Library
- *The Man Who Was Poe,* Avi, Audio Bookshelf
- *The Roald Dahl Audio Collection: A Great Favorite,* Caedmon Audio Cassette
- *Wayside School Gets a Little Stranger,* Louis Sachar, Random House

BOOKS ON VIDEOTAPE

Videotapes of children's literature provide opportunities for struggling readers to view a story before reading it; compare the two different mediums (movie and book); or simply have a background knowledge that will help them predict words, understand events, and be familiar with characters when they read the same book. A list of available videotapes include:

- *The Baby-Sitters Club,* Ann M. Martin
- *James and the Giant Peach,* Roald Dahl

- *Matilda*, Roald Dahl
- *Dr. Seuss's ABC*, Dr. Seuss
- *Horton Hatches the Egg*, Dr. Seuss
- *How the Grinch Stole Christmas*, Dr. Seuss
- *My Many Colored Days*, Dr. Seuss
- *Green Eggs and Ham*, Dr. Seuss
- *Are You My Mother?*, P. D. Eastman
- *Goosebumps: Night of the Living Dummy*, R. L. Steine
- *The Lion, the Witch, and the Wardrobe*, C. S Lewis
- *Yo! Yes?*, Chris Raschka
- *Fly Away Home*, Eve Bunting, Reading Rainbow

BOOKS AVAILABLE IN SPANISH

There are many children's books that are available in Spanish. The following list includes those that are summarized in chapter 4. For a more complete list of available books see *Lectorum: The Best in Children's Literature in Spanish and English for Grades PreK–8* (2002), Lectorum Publications, Inc. 205 Chubb Avenue, Lyndhurst, NJ 07071-3520.

Picture Books

- *I Like Me*, Nancy Carlson
- *Tea with Milk*, Allen Say
- *Chicken Sunday*, Patricia Polacco
- *Pink and Say*, Patricia Polacco
- *Green Eggs and Ham*, Dr. Seuss
- *Oh, The Places You'll Go!*, Dr. Seuss

Short Chapter Books/Short Novels

- *Bunnicula: A Rabbit-Tale of Mystery*, Deborah and James Howe
- *The Time Warp Trio Books*, Jon Scieszka
- *Sarah, Plain and Tall*, Patricia MacLachlan
- *Goosebumps Series*, R. L. Stein
- *Seedfolks*, Paul Fleischman

Longer Fiction

- *Hatchet,* Gary Paulsen
- *Nightjohn,* Gary Paulsen
- *James and the Giant Peach,* Roald Dahl
- *Harry Potter and the Sorcerer's Stone,* J. K. Rowling
- *Superfudge,* Judy Blume
- *Scorpions,* Walter Dean Myers

CHILDREN'S MAGAZINES

Children's magazines contain well-written short stories and quality illustrations, include educational games and activities, and present opportunities for struggling readers to read magazines along with parents and caregivers. Many quality children's magazines are available that pertain to specific interests (e.g., science, math, sports, outdoor adventure) and age levels. The following list includes this wide variety.

- *Cricket, the Magazine for Children,* P.O. Box 52961, Boulder, CO 80322-2961 (ages 2–12)
- *Chickadee,* Young Naturalist Foundation, P.O. Box 11314, Des Moines, IA 50340 (ages 4–9, story magazine)
- *Cobblestone: The History Magazine for Young People,* Cobblestone Publishing, Inc., 30 Grove Street, Peterborough, NH 03458 (ages 7–12)
- *Cyberkids,* http://www.cyberkids.com/ (A magazine for children that asks readers to contribute their own writing and art work)
- *DynaMath,* Scholastic, Inc., 730 Broadway, New York, NY 10003 (ages 7–12)
- *Highlights for Children,* 2300 West Fifth Avenue, Columbus, OH 43272-0002 (ages 2–12; stories, poems, activities, puzzles)
- *HiP Magazine,* www.hipmag.org, 510-848-9650 (addresses educational, emotional and social needs of deaf and hard-of-hearing children)
- *Ladybug,* Cricket Country Lane, Box 50284, Boulder, CO 80321–0284 (ages 4–9, story magazine)
- *National Geographic World,* National Geographic Society, 17th and M Streets NW, Washington, DC 20036 (ages 7–12; natural history, outdoor adventure, science, sports, astronomy)
- *Odyssey,* Kalmbach Publishing Co., P.O. Box 1612, Waukesha WI 53187 (ages 7–12)

- *National Geographic for Kids,* http://www.nationalgeographic.com/ng-forkids/, National Geographic Society (newest magazine published by the National Geographic Society that is for classroom use to improve nonficton literacy skills)
- *Ranger Rick,* National Wildlife Federation, 1400 16th Street NW, Washington, DC 20036-2266 (ages 7–12, animals, nature, science, astronomy)
- *Sesame Street Magazine,* Children's Television Workshop, One Lincoln Plaza, New York, NY 10023 (ages 4–9, story magazine)
- *Sports Illustrated for Kids,* Time Inc., Time & Life Building, Rockefeller Center, New York, NY 10020–1393 (ages 7–12, sports)
- *Stone Soup,* http://www.stonesoupo.com/ (an international magazine for readers up to age 13; children may send in their own stories and poems)

BOOK CLUBS

Book clubs support school programs and provide opportunities for home literacy. *Scholastic at Home Book Clubs* (Grolier.com) offers book selections for grades PreK–1, 2–3, and 4–6 (http://teacher.scholastic.com/clubs). Planet Troll, another well known school-based book club, has online information at http://www.troll.com.

TELEVISION PROGRAMS THAT PROMOTE LITERACY

Television programs provide opportunities for readers to hear quality children's literature and to develop word recognition and listening comprehension skills. Several programs feature celebrities reading quality children's picture books like *Kino's Storytime* and *The Reading Rainbow.* Others feature book characters such as Clifford the Big Red Dog and Arthur or extend series books like *Goosebumps* and *The Nightmare Room.* In *The Magic School Bus* programs, viewers will see the wondrous science teacher, Ms. Frizzle, directing her students to faraway places for observation and discovery. *Sesame Street* provides opportunities for emergent readers to develop word recognition skills and basic concepts in the company of magical creatures and familiar friends. Here are a few favorites:

- *Reading Rainbow* (authors and celebrities read picture books)
- *Kino's Storytime* (celebrities read picture books, www.pbs.org/storytime)
- *Sesame Street* (http://www.sesameworkshop.org/sesamestreet/)
- *Clifford The Big Red Dog* (PBS KIDS http://pbskids.org/clifford/)
- *Arthur* (Channel 11)
- *Goosebumps* (Fox Family Channel, www.scholastic.com/goosebumps/)
- *The Nightmare Room* (live action TV series, www.sthenightmareroom. com/)
- *The Magic School Bus* (Fox Kids TV)
- *WISHBONE Series* (introduces children to classic literature through a terrier named Jack Russell—PBS)

SOFTWARE FOR CHILDREN

Software programs provide entertainment and motivation while promoting literacy skills. *Dr. Seuss Kindergarten* (Broderbund Softward) includes 250 activities that teach phonics, language-related skills, and math and measurement (ages 4–6) (http://www.broderbund.com). Several interactive programs focus on characters in popular children's book series. In *The American Girls Premiere* (the Learning Company), the five American Girls create their own historical dramas. (See the Web site that expands on chapter book stories and that has a fan club at http://www.americangirl.com/.) *The Magic School Bus* software includes *The Magic School Bus Explores Inside the Earth, The Magic School Bus Explores the Solar System,* and *The Magic School Bus Explores the Ocean.* See the Web site at http://scholastic.com/Magic-SchoolBus/index.htm. Software for Marc Brown's popular *Arthur* picture books includes *Arthur's 1st Grade* (the Learning Company). The Arthur Page Web site is maintained by PBS at http://www.pbs.org/wgbh/arthur/. Nancy Drew software includes *Nancy Drew Stay Tuned for Danger* and *Nancy Drew Secrets Can Kill.*

WEB SITES FOR CHILDREN

- **http://www.ala.org** (American Library Association). Provides links to ALA Resources for Parents, Teens and Kids with links to Cool Sites for Kids; Kids Connect Favorite Websites; Notable Children's Web Sites;

700 + Amazing, Spectacular, Mysterious, Wonderful Web Sites for Kids and the Adults Who Care About Them.

- **http://www.nationalgeographic.com/ngforkids/.** This is the online edition of *National Geographic for Kids* that features articles, interactive games, and information for parents and teachers.
- **www.bookadventure.org** (The book Adventure Web Site). Children create their own book lists from more than 5,400 recommended titles, take quizzes on their books, and earn points toward prizes.

AUTHOR WEB SITES

- **David Adler,** http://www.edupaperback.org/authorbios/Adler David.html
- **Avi,** http://www.avi-writer.com/
- **Judy Blume,** http://www.judyblume.com/
- **Betsy Byars,** http://www.betsybyars.com/
- **Roald Dahl,** http://www.roalddahl.com/
- **Virginia Hamilton,** http://www.virginiahamilton.com/
- **S. E. Hinton,** http://www.sehinton.com/
- **Mary Pope Osborn,** http://www.randomhouse.com/kids/ magictreehouse/books/books.html
- **Katherine Paterson,** http://www.terabithia.com/
- **Patricia Polacco,** http://www.patriciapolacco.com/
- **Allen Say,** http://wwweduplace.com/rdg/author/say/index.html
- **Jon Scieszka and Lane Smith,** http://www.chucklebait.com/
- **Dr. Seuss,** http://www.randomhouse.com/seussville/
- **Lemony Snicket,** http://www.kidsreads.com/features/010314-lemony-snicket.asp and www.lemonysnicket.com/
- **Jerry Spinelli,** http://www.carr.lib.md.as/authco/spinelli-j.htm/
- **R. L. Stine's** *Goosebumps,* www.scholastic.com/goosebumps/; and *The Nightmare Room,* www.thenightmareroom.com/

ADDITIONAL WEB SITES

- **http://www.ala.org/** (American Library Association): Includes link For Parents and Others with links to Born to Read: How to Raise a Reader; For Parents and Caregivers (links to parenting resources); Kids Connect @The Library: Tips For Parents (tips on how to raise a reader and make

the most of the library); and Learning Disabilities—Early Warning Signs.
- **www.amazon.com:** Information about books in print, authors, and how to order books.
- **http://trelease-on-reading.com:** Information on reading books aloud to children by noted educator and author Jim Trelease.
- **www.ed.gov/pubs/parents/Reading/Postscripts.html:** Suggestions for helping older children become fluent readers.
- **www.google.com:** A good search engine that provides easy access to information (e.g., locates books, children's authors, and other topics related to literacy).
- **http://www.ed.gov/pubs/parents:** Provides literacy information for parents and caregivers.
- **http://readingpath.org** (The Reading Pathfinder Web Site): Identifies and selects the best resources available to answer reading-related questions posed by parents and educators (U.S. Department of Education through the ERIC Clearinghouse on Elementary and Early Childhood Education).
- **http://www.school.discovery.com.** This is an educational link for parent, teachers, and students.
- **http://www.brainsarefun.com/Books.html:** Provides a brief list of books to read aloud to your children, ages birth through 18.

PROFESSIONAL RESOURCES

The following professional resources include books and handbooks specifically for parents and caregivers who support reading and provide resources for selecting children's literature.

Anderson, R. et al. *Becoming a Nation of Readers: The Report of the Commission on Reading.* (1985).Washington, DC: National Academy of Education, National Institute of Education, Center for the Study of Reading.

Calkins, L. (1997). *Raising Lifelong Learners: A Parent's Guide.* Reading, MA: Perseus Books.

Cullinan, B. (1992). *Read to Me: Raising Kids Who Love to Read.*

Hearne, B. *Choosing books for children.* (2002) NY Delacorte Press.

Kimmel, M. M. (1998). *For Reading Out Loud: A Guide to Sharing Books with Children.* NY: Delacorte Press.

Larrick, N. *A Parent's Guide to Children's Reading* (5th Ed.). NY: Bantam Books.

Lewis, V., and Mayes, W. (1998). *Valerie & Walter's Best Books for Children.* NY: Avon Books.

What Parents Need to Know. A handbook describing literacy development created by New Standards, a joint program of the Learning Research and Development Center of the University of Pittsburgh and the National Center on Education and the Economy (NCEE). For free copies, email info@ncee.org. (http://www.ncee.org/ourProducts/catalogOverview.html)

Lipson, R.E. (1991). *The New York Times Parent's Guide to the Best Books for Children.* NY: Random House.

Trelease, J. (2001). *The Read-Aloud Handbook* (5th Ed.). NY: Penguin Group.

PROFESSIONAL ORGANIZATIONS AND SERVICES

Professional organizations and services support parents and caregivers and provide opportunities for involvement. The following organizations provide information and support for teachers, parents, and caregivers with children who have special learning needs.

Children and Adults with Attention Deficit Disorder, 499 N.W 70th Avenue, Suite 308, Plantation, FL 38817

Orton Dyslexia Society, Chester Building Suite 382, Baltimore, MD 21204

The International Dyslexia Association (IDA), an international organization for teachers and parents with dyslexia and related difficulties in learning to read and write, www.interdys.org, 410-296-0232

National Center for Learning Disabilities (NCLD), a national organization for teachers and parents, www.LD.org, 888-575-7373 (toll free)

Schwab Learning, an online guide developed by the Charles and Helen Schwab Foundation that is especially for parents of children newly identified learning disablities, www.schwablearning.org, 650-655-2410

Parent Advocacy Coalition for Educational Rights Center (PACER), a parent organization created by parents of children with disabilities to help other families with similar challenges, www.pacer.org

Book Titles by Genre

PICTURE BOOKS (FICTION/NONFICTION)

A Blue Butterfly, A Story About Claude Monet, Bijou Le Tord (1995)

A Day in the Life of a Dancer, Linda Hayward (2001) (Dorling Kindersley Readers)

A Fine, Fine School, Sharon Creech (2001)

Amelia Bedelia, Peggy Parish (1963)

Are You My Mother?, P. D. Eastman (1960,1988)

Chicken Sunday, Patricia Polacco (1992)

Dance!, Elisha Cooper (2001)

Dance, Bill T. Jones and Susan Kuklin (1998).

Diego, Jeanette and Jonah Winter (1991)

Ed Emberley's Big Purple Drawing Book, Ed Emberly (1981).

Flower Garden, Eve Bunting, illustrated by Kathryn Hewitt (1994)

Fly Away Home, Eve Bunting (1991) (ALA Notable Book)

Franciso Goya, Mike Venezia (1991)

Gleam and Glow, Eve Bunting (2001)

Go, Dog. Go!, P. D. Eastman (1961)

Going Home, Eve Bunting, illustrated by David Diaz (1996)

Grandfather's Journey, written and illustrated by Allen Say (1993) (Caldecott Medal)

Green Eggs and Ham, Dr. Seuss (1960)

Hoops with Swoopes, Susan Kuklin and Sheryl Swoopes (2001)

I Dreamed I Was a Ballerina, Anna Pavolva, illustrated by Edgar Degas (2001)

I Have an Olive Tree, Eve Bunting, illustrated by Karen Barbour (1999)

I Like Me, Nancy Carlson (1988)

Leonardo's Horse, Jean Fritz (2001)

Martin's Big Words: The Life of Dr. Martin Luther King, Jr., Doreen Rappaport (2001)

My Many Colored Days, Dr. Seuss (1966)

My Secret Camera: Life in the Lodz Ghetto, photographs by Mendel Grossman, text by Frank Dabba Smith (2000)

Oh, the Places You'll Go!, Dr. Seuss (1990)

Paul Gauguin, Mike Venezia (1993)

Pink and Say, Patricia Polacco (1994)

Red-Eyed Tree Frog, Joy Cowley, photographs by Nic Bishop (1999)

Sam and the Tigers, Julius Lester, illustrated by Jerry Pinkney (1996)

Shooting for the Moon: The Amazing Life and Times of Annie Oakley, Stephen Krensky (2001)

Smoky Night, Eve Bunting (1994) (Caldecott Medal)

Tea with Milk, Allen Say (1999)

Thank You, Mr. Falker, Patricia Polacco (1998)

The Cat in the Hat, Dr. Seuss (1957)

The Dance, Richard Paul Evans, illustrated by Jonathan Linton (1999)

The Dinosaurs of Waterhouse Hawkins, Barbara Kerley (2001)

The Little Ballerina, Sally Grindley (1999) (Eyewitness Readers)

The Stray Dog, Marc Simont (2001)

The Wall, Eve Bunting (1990) (ALA Notable Book)

Tree of Cranes, Allen Say (1991)

Yo! Yes?, Chris Raschka (1993) (Caldecott Honor)

Wings, Christopher Myers (2000)

SHORT CHAPTER BOOKS (FICTION/NONFICTION) AND SHORT NOVELS (UNDER 100 PAGES)

A Lion to Guard Us, Clyde Bulla (1981)

A Mouse Called Wolf, Dick King-Smith (1997)

Aunt Eater Loves a Mystery, Doug Cushman (1987)

Billy the Bird, Dick King-Smith (2001)

Bunnicula: A Rabbit-Tale of Mystery, Deborah and James Howe (1979)

Cam Jansen and the Catnapping Mystery, David Adler (1998)

Detective Dinosaur Lost and Found, James Skofield (1998)

Encyclopedia Brown and the Case of the Mysterious Handprints, Donald Sobol (1985)

Encyclopedia Brown and the Case of the Slippery Salamander, Donald Sobol (2000)

Finding Providence: The Story of Roger Williams, Avi (1997)

Freckle Juice, Judy Blume (1971)

Free at Last! The Story of Martin Luther King, Jr., Angela Bull (2000)

Ghost Town at Sundown, Mary Pope Osborne (1997)

How to Eat Fried Worms, Thomas Rockwell (1973)

I Can't Accept Not Trying: Michael Jordan on the Pursuit of Excellence, Michael Jordan (1994)

In a Dark, Dark Room and Other Scary Stories, retold by Alvin Schwartz (1984) (An I Can Read Book)

In Aunt Lucy's Kitchen—The Cobble Street Cousins, Cynthia Rylant (1998)

Love That Dog, Sharon Creech (2001)

Jane On Her Own: A Catwings Tale, Ursula K. LeGuin (1999)

Marvin Redpost A Magic Crystal?, Louis Sachar (2000)

Marvin Redpost Alone in His Teacher's House, Louis Sachar (2000)

Marvin Redpost Is He A Girl?, Louis Sachar (1993)

Marvin's Best Christmas Present, Katherine Paterson (1997)

Mouse Soup, Arnold Lobel (1977)

Mouse Tales, Arnold Lobel (1972)

More Scary Stories to Tell in the Dark, retold by Alvin Schwartz (1984)

Mr. Putter and Tabby Paint the Porch, Cynthia Rylant (2000)

Nate the Great and the Monster Mess, Marjorie Seinman Sharmant (1999)

NFL's Greatest Upsets, James Buckley, Jr. (2000)

Owl at Home, Arnold Lobel (1975)

Poppleton in Fall, Cynthia Rylant (1999)

Poppleton in Spring, Cynthia Rylant (1999)

Robert Clemente, James Buckley, Jr. (2001)

Sarah, Plain and Tall, Patricia MacLachlan (1985) (Newbery Medal)

Seedfolks, Paul Fleischman (1997)

Shoeshine Girl, C. Bulla (1975)

Spider Kane and the Mystery at Jumbo Nightcrawler's, Mary Pope Osborne (1999)

Strikeout Kings, James Buckley, Jr. (2001)

Summer Party—The Cobble Street Cousins, Cynthia Rylant (2001)

The Golly Sisters Go West, Betsy Byars (1985)

The High-Rise Private Eyes: The Case of the Puzzling Possum, Cynthia Rylant (2001)

The Imp That Ate My Homework, Lawrence Yep (1998)

The Josefina Story Quilt, Eleanor Coerr (1986)

The King's Equal, Katherine Paterson (1992)

The Lucky Lottery, A to Z Mysteries, Ron Roy (2000)

The Panther Mystery: The Boxcar Children, Gerturde C. Warner (1998)
The Skirt, Gary Soto (1992)
The Stone Fox, John Reynolds Gardiner (1980)
The Sword in the Tree, Clyde Bulla (1956)
The Time Warp Trio: It's All Greek to Me, Jon Scieszka (1999)
The Time Warp Trio: See You Later, Gladiator, Jon Scieszka (2000)
The Time Warp Trio: Summer Reading Is Killing Me!, Jon Scieszka (1998)
The Zack Files: The Boy Who Cried Bigfoot, Dan Greenburg (2000)

NONFICTION (100–250 PAGES)

Dinosaurs, Magic Tree House Research Guide, Will Osborne and Mary Pope Osborne (2000)
Mummies and Pyramids, Magic Tree House Research Guide, Will Osborne and Mary Pope Osborne (2001)

FICTION (100–250 PAGES)

A Series of Unfortunate Events: The Bad Beginning, Lemony Snicket (1999)
A Year Down Yonder, Richard Peck (2000) (Newbery Award)
An Island Like You: Stories of the Barrio, Judith Ortiz Cofer (1995) (ALA Best Book for Young Adults, Pura Belpre Award)
Baseball in April and Other Short Stories, Gary Soto (1990) (ALA Best Book for Young Adults)
Blackwater, Eve Bunting (1999) (ALA Quick Picks for Reluctant Young Adult Readers, 2000)
Bluish, Virginia Hamilton (1999)
Bunnicula Strikes Again!, James Howe (1999)
Brian's Return, Gary Paulsen (1999) (ALA Quick Picks for Reluctant Young Adult Readers, 2000)
Brian's Winter, Gary Paulsen (1996)
Claudia's Big Party—The Baby-Sitters Club, Ann M. Martin (1998)
Coffin on a Case, Eve Bunting (1992)
Dead Letter: A Herculeah Jones Mystery, Betsy Byars (1996) (IRA Children's Choice Book)
Dew Drop Dead, James Howe (1990)
Ella Enchanted, Gail Carson Levine (1997) (Newbery Honor)
Ghosts I Have Been, Richard Peck (1977)

Hatchet, Gary Paulsen (1987) (Newbery Honor)

Help! I'm Trapped in My Teacher's Body!, Todd Strasser (1993)

Help! I'm Trapped in a Vampire's Body!, Todd Strasser (2000)

Holes, Louis Sachar (1998)

James and the Giant Peach, Roald Dahl (1961)

Joey Pigza Loses Control, Jack Gantos (2000) (Newbery Honor)

Joey Pigza Swallowed the Key, Jack Gantos (1998) (ALA Notable Children's Book)

Just Ella, Margaret Peterson Haddix (1999) (ALA Quick Picks for Reluctant Young Adult Readers, 2000)

Maniac Magee, Jerry Spinelli (1990) (Newbery Award)

Midnight Magic, Avi (1999) (ALA Quick Picks for Reluctant Young Adult Readers, 2000)

Nightjohn, Avi (1993)

Poppy, Avi (1996) (ALA Notable Book)

Run Billy, Run, Matt Christopher (1980)

Running Out of Time, Margaret Peterson Haddix (1995)

Scare School, The Nightmare Room Series, R. L. Stine (2001)

Scorpions, Walter Dean Myers (1988) (Newbery Honor)

Snowboard Maverick, Matt Christopher (1997)

Something Upstairs, Avi (1997)

Superfudge, Judy Blume (1980)

Taking Sides, Gary Soto (1991)

The Barn, Avi (1994)

The Case of the Lion Dance, Lawrence Yep (1998)

The Ghost Belonged to Me, Richard Peck (1975)

The Fighting Ground, Avi (1984)

The Haunting Hour, R. L. Stine (2001)

The Laundry News, Andrew Clements (1999)

The Secrets of Droon: Under the Serpent Sea, Tony Abbott (2001)

The Skin I'm In, Sharon G. Flake (1998) (Coretta Scott King Award, 1999; ALA Quick Picks for Reluctant Young Adult Readers, 1999)

The True Confession of Charlotte Doyle, Avi (1990)

Tom, Babette, & Simon: Three Tales of Transformation, Avi (1995)

Wayside School Gets a Little Stranger, Louis Sachar (1995)

What Do Fish Have to Do with Anything?, Avi (1997)

Who Stole the Wizard of Oz?, Avi (1981)

Wringer, Jerry Spinelli (1997) (Newbery Honor)

FICTION (250–310 PAGES)

Esperanza Rising, Pam Muñoz Ryan (2000)
Harry Potter and the Sorcerer's Stone, J. K. Rowling (1998)
Monster, Walter Dean Myers (1999) (National Book Award Finalist; Michael
   L. Printz Award; ALA Quick Picks for Reluctant Young Adult Readers,
   2000)
Slam, Walter Dean Myers (1996) (Coretta Scott King Award)

POETRY

A Light in the Attic, Shel Silverstein (1981)
A Pizza the Size of the Sun, Jack Prelutsky (1994) (ALA Notable Book)
Brown Angels, Walter Dean Myers (1993)
Casey at the Bat: A Ballad of the Republic Sung in the Year 1888, Christopher
   Bing (2000) (Caldecott Honor)
Everett Anderson's Goodbye, Lucille Clifton (1983) (Coretta Scott King
   Award)
Extra Innings: Baseball Poems, selected by Lee Bennett Hopkins (1993)
Falling Up, Shel Silverstein (1996)
For Laughing Out Loud: Poems to Tickle Your Funnybone, Jack Prelutsky
   (1991)
If Pigs Could Fly . . . And Other Deep Thoughts, Bruce Lansky (2000)
Insect Soup: Bug Poems, Barry Louis Polisar (1999)
No More Homework! No More Tests! Kids' Favorite Funny School Poems, se-
   lected by Bruce Lansky (1997)
Quiet Storm: Voices of Young Black Poets, selected by Lydia Omolola Oku-
   toro (1999) (ALA Quick Picks for Reluctant Young Adult Readers, 2000)
Salting the Ocean: 100 Poems by Young Poets, selected by Naomi Shihab Nye
   (2000)
Sports! Sports! Sports! A Poetry Collection, selected by Lee Bennett Hopkins
   (1999)
The Basket Counts, Arnold Adoff (2000)
Where The Sidewalk Ends, Shel Silverstein (1974)

Book Titles by Interest

ADVENTURE/SURVIVAL

Picture Books

Gleam and Glow, Eve Bunting (2001)
Shooting for the Moon: The Amazing Life and Times of Annie Oakley, Stephen
   Krensky (2001)

Fiction

Brian's Return, Gary Paulsen (1999) (ALA Quick Picks for Reluctant Young
   Readers/2000)
Brian's Winter, Gary Paulsen (1996)
Hatchet, Gary Paulsen (1987) (Newbery Honor)
Holes, Louis Sachar (1998) (Newbery Award)
Maniac Magee, Jerry Spinelli (1990) (Newbery Award)
Midnight Magic, Avi (1999)
Running Out of Time, Margaret Peterson Haddix (1995)
Stone Fox, John Reynolds Gardiner (1980)
The True Confessions of Charlotte Doyle, Avi (1990)

ANIMALS

Picture Books

Go, Dog. Go!, P. D. Eastman (1961)
Sam and the Tigers, Julius Lester (1996)

The Cat in the Hat, Dr. Seuss (1957)
The Stray Dog, March Simont (2001)

Easy Reading Books

A Mouse Called Wolf, Dick King-Smith (1997)
Mouse Soup, Arnold Lobel (1977)
Mouse Tales, Arnold Lobel (1972)
Mr. Putter & Tabby Paint the Porch, Cynthia Rylant (2000)
Owl at Home, Arnold Lobel (1975)
Poppleton in Fall, Cynthia Rylant (1999)
Poppleton in Spring, Cynthia Rylant (1999)

Fiction

Bunnicula: A Rabbit-Tale of Mystery, Deborah and James Howe (1979)
Bunnicula Strikes Again!, James Howe (1999)
Pets, in *What Do Fish Have to Do with Anything and Other Stories,* Avi
    (1997)
Poppy, Avi (1996)
The High-Rise Private Eyes: The Case of the Puzzling Possum, Cynthia Ry-
    lant (2001)
The Stone Fox, John Reynolds Gardiner (1980)

ART

Picture Books

A Blue Butterfly: A Story About Claude Monet, Bijou Le Tord (1995)
Diego, Jeanette and Jonah Winter (1991)
Ed Emberley's Big Purple Drawing Book, Ed Emberley (1981)
Franciso Goya, Mike Venezia (1991)
I Dreamed I Was a Ballerina, Anna Pavlova, illustrated by Edgar Degas
    (2001)
Leonardo's Horse, Jean Fritz (2001)
Paul Gauguin, Mike Venezia (1993)
The Dinosaurs of Waterhouses Hawkins, Barbara Kerley (2001)

BIOGRAPHY

Picture Books

Diego, Jeanette and Jonah Winter (1991)
Franciso Goya, Mike Venezia (1991)
Leonardo's Horse, Jean Fritz (2001)
Martin's Big Words: The Life of Dr. Martin Luther King, Jr., Doreen Rappaport (2001)
Paul Gauguin, Mike Venezia (1993)
Shooting for the Moon: The Amazing Life and Times of Annie Oakley, Stephen Krensky (2001)
The Dinoaurs of Waterhouse Hawkins, Barbara Kerley (2001)

Easy Reading Books

Free At Last! The Story of Martin Luther King, Jr., Angela Bull (2000)
Strikeout Kings, James Buckley, Jr. (2001)

DANCE

Picture Books

Dance!, Elisha Cooper (2001)
Dance, Bill T. Jones (1998)
I Dreamed I Was a Ballerina, Anna Pavolva, illustrated by Edgar Degas (2001)
The Dance, Richard Paul Evans (1999)

Easy Reading Books

The Little Ballerina, Sally Grindley (1999) (Eyewitness Readers)
A Day in the Life of a Dancer, Linda Hayward (2001)

FAMILY RELATIONSHIPS

Picture Books

Flower Garden, Eve Bunting (1994)

Fly Away Home, Eve Bunting (1991)
Gleam and Glow, Eve Bunting (2001)
Grandfather's Journey, Allen Say (1993) (Caldecott Medal)
Tea with Milk, Allen Say (1999)
The Wall, Eve Bunting (1990)
Tree of Cranes, Allen Say (1991)

Easy Reading Books

In Aunt Lucy's Kitchen—The Cobble Street Cousins, Cynthia Rylant (1998)
Marvin's Best Christmas Present Ever, Katherine Paterson (1997)
Summer Party—The Cobble Street Cousins, Cynthia Rylant (2001)
The Josefina Story Quilt, Eleanor Coerr (1986)

Fiction

Esperanza Rising, Pam Muñoz Ryan (2000)
Mother and Daughter (pp. 60–68) from *Baseball in April and Other Stories,*
    Gary Soto (1990)
Stone Fox, John Reynolds Gardiner (1980)
Superfudge, Judy Blume (1980)
The Barn, Avi (1994)
The Skin I'm In, Sharon G. Flake (1998) (Coretta Scott King Award, 1999)

FANTASY

Picture Books

Go, Dog. Go!, P. D. Eastman (1961)
Green Eggs and Ham, Dr. Seuss (1960)
I Like Me, Nancy Carlson (1988)
Oh, The Places You'll Go!, Dr. Seuss (1990)
Sam and the Tigers, Julius Lester (1996)
The Cat in the Hat, Dr. Seuss (1957)

Easy Reading Books

A Mouse Called Wolf, Dick King-Smith (1997)
Aunt Eater Loves A Mystery, Doug Cushman (1987)

Billy the Bird, Dick King-Smith (2001)
Detective Dinosaur Lost and Found, James Skofield (1998)
Ghost Town at Sundown, Mary Pope Osborne (1997)
In a Dark, Dark Room and Other Scary Stories, retold by Alvin Swartz (1984)
Jane on Her Own: A Catwings Tale, Ursula K. Le Guin (1999)
Marvin Redpost A Magic Crystal?, Louis Sachar (2000)
Marvin Redpost Alone in His Teacher's House, Louis Sachar (1994)
Marvin Redpost Is He a Girl?, Louis Sachar (1993)
More Scary Stories to Tell in the Dark, retold by Alvin Swartz (1984)
Mouse Soup, Arnold Lobel (1977)
Mouse Tales, Arnold Lobel (1972)
Own at Home, Arnold Lobel (1975)
Poppleton in Fall, Cynthia Rylant (1999)
Poppleton in Spring, Cynthia Rylant (1999)
Spider Kane and the Mystery at Jumbo Nightcrawler's, Mary Pope Osborne
    (1999)
The High-Rise Private Eyes: the Case of the Puzzling Possum, Cynthia Rylant
    (2001)
The Imp That Ate My Homework, Lawrence Yep (1998)
The King's Equal, Katherine Paterson (1992),
The Time Warp Trio: It's All Greek to Me, Jon Scieszka (1999)
The Time Warp Trio: See You Later, Gladiator, Jon Scieszka (2000)
The Time Warp Trio: Summer Reading Is Killing Me!, Jon Scieszka (1998)
The Zack Files: The Boy Who Cried Bigfoot, Dan Greenburg (2000)

Fiction

A Series of Unfortunate Events: The Bad Beginning, Lemony Snicket (1999)
Bunnicula: A Rabbit-Tale of Mystery, Deborah and James Howe (1979)
Bunnicula Strikes Again, James Howe (1999)
Ella Enchanted, Gail Carson Levine (1997)
Ghosts I Have Been, Richard Peck (1977)
Harry Potter and the Sorcerer's Stone, J. K. Rowling (1998)
Holes, Louis Sachar (1998) (Newbery Award)
Help! I'm Trapped in My Teacher's Body!, Todd Strasser (1993)
Help! I'm Trapped in a Vampire's Body!, Todd Strsser (2000)
James and the Giant Peach, Roald Dahl (1961)
Just Ella, Margaret Peterson Haddix (1999)
Maniac Magee, Jerry Spinelli (1990) (Newbery Award)

Midnight Magic, Avi (1999)
Poppy, Avi (1996)
Running Out of Time, Margaret Peterson Haddix (1995)
Scare School, the Nightmare Room Series, R. L. Stine (2001)
Something Upstairs, Avi (1997)
The Ghost Belonged to Me, Richard Peck (1975)
The Haunting Hour: Chills in the Dead of the Night, R. L. Stine (2001)
The Secrets of Droon: Under the Serpent Sea, Tony Abbott (2001)
Tom, Babette, & Simon: Three Tales of Transformation, Avi (1995)
Wayside School Gets a Little Stranger, Louis Sachar (1995)

FRIENDSHIP

Picture Books

Chicken Sunday, Patricia Polacco (1992)
Smoky Night, Eve Bunting, illustrated by Diad Diaz (1994) (Caldecott Medal)
Yo! Yes?, Chris Raschka (1993) (Caldecott Honor)

Easy Reading Books

A Mouse Called Wolf, Dick King-Smith (1997)
In Aunt Lucy's Kitchen—The Cobble Street Cousins, Cynthia Rylant (1998)
Shoeshine Girl, C. Bulla (1975)
Summer Party—The Cobble Street Cousins, Cynthia Rylant (2001)

Fiction

Baseball in April and Other Short Stories, Gary Soto (1990)
Bluish, Virginia Hamilton (1999)
Brian's Return, Gary Paulsen (1999)
Claudia's Big Party—The Baby-Sitters Club, Ann M. Martin (1998)
Maniac Magee, Jerry Spinelli (1990) (Newbery Award)
Scorpions, Walter Dean Myers (1988) (Newbery Honor)
Slam, Walter Dean Myers (1996) (Coretta Scott King Award)
Stone Fox, John Reynolds Gariner (1980)
Superfudge, Judy Blume (1980)
Taking Sides, Gary Soto (1991)

The Skin I'm In, Sharon Flake (1998) (Coretta Scott King Award)
The Skirt, Gary Soto (1992)

GHOSTS

Easy Reading Books

Ghost Town at Sundown, Mary Pope Osborne (1997)
In a Dark, Dark Room and Other Scary Stories, retold by Alvin Schwartz (1984)
More Scary Stories to Tell in the Dark, retold by Alvin Schwartz (1984)

Fiction

Ghosts I Have Been, Richard Peck (1977)
Midnight Magic, Avi (1999)
Pets, in *What Do Fish Have to Do with Anything?,* Avi (1997)
Something Upstairs, Avi (1997)
The Ghost Belonged to Me, Richard Peck (1975)
The Haunting Hour, R. L. Stine (2001)

HISTORICAL FICTION

Picture Books

Gleam and Glow, Eve Bunting (2001)
Minty: A Story of Young Harriet Tubman, Alan Schroeder (1996)
Pink and Say, Patricia Polacco (1994)

Easy Reading Books

A Lion to Guard Us, Clyde Bulla (1981)
Finding Providence: The Story of Roger Williams, Avi (1997)
Sarah, Plain and Tall, Patricia MacLachlan (1985) (Newbery Medal)
The Josefina Story Quilt, Eleanor Coerr (1986)
The Sword in the Tree, Clyde Bulla (1956)

Fiction

A Year Down Yonder, Richard Peck (2000) (Newbery Award)
Esperanza Rising, Pam Muñoz Ryan (2000)
Nightjohn, Gary Paulsen (1993)
The Barn, Avi (1994)
The Fighting Ground, Avi (1984)
The True Confessions of Charlotte Doyle, Avi (1990) (Newbery Honor)

HUMOR

Picture Books

A Fine, Fine School, Sharon Creech (2001)
Are You My Mother?, P. D. Eastman (1960, 1988)
Green Eggs and Ham, Dr. Seuss (1960)
I Like Me, Nancy Carlson (1988)
Oh, the Places You'll Go!, Dr. Seuss (1990)
The Cat in the Hat, Dr. Seuss (1957)

Easy Reading Books

Amelia Bedelia, Peggy Parish (1963)
Aunt Eater Loves A Mystery, Doug Cushman (1987)
Detective Dinosaur Lost and Found, James Skofield (1998)
Marvin Redpost A Magic Crystal, Louis Sachar (2000)
Marvin Redpost Alone in His Teacher's House, Louis Sachar (1994)
Marvin Redpost Is He a Girl?, Louis Sachar (1993)
Mouse Soup, Arnold Lobel (1977)
Mouse Tales, Arnold Lobel (1972)
Mr. Putter & Tabby Paint the Porch, Cynthia Rylant (2000)
Poppleton in Fall, Cynthia Rylant (1999)
Poppleton in Spring, Cynthia Rylant (1999)
The Golly Sisters Go West, Betsy Byars (1985)
The Imp That Ate My Homework, Lawrence Yep (1998)
The Time Warp Trio It's All Greek to Me, Jon Scieszka (1999)
The Zack Files, Dan Greenburg (2000)

Poetry

If Pigs Could Fly . . . And Other Deep Thoughts, Bruce Lansky (2000)
Insect Soup: Bug Poems, Barry Louis Polisar (1999)
No More Homework! No More Tests! Kids Favorite Funny School Poems,
   selected by Bruce Lansky (1997)

Fiction

A Year Down Yonder, Richard Peck (2000) (Newbery Award)
Bunnicula: A Rabbit-Tale of Mystery, Deborah and James Howe (1979)
Bunnicula Strikes Again!, James Howe (1999)
Freckle Juice, Judy Blume (1971)
Help! I'm Trapped in my Teacher's Body!, Todd Strasser (1993)
Help! I'm Trapped in a Vampire's Body!, Todd Strasser (2000)
How to Eat Fried Worms, Thomas Rockwell (1973)
Love That Dog, Sharon Creech (2001)
Superfudge, Judy Blume (1980)
Wayside School Gets a Little Stranger, Louis Sachar (1995)

IDENTITY/SOLVING PROBLEMS

Picture Books

I Like Me!, Nancy Carlson (1988)
Oh, the Places You'll Go!, Dr. Seuss (1990)
Thank you, Mr. Falker, Particia Polacco (1998)
Wings, Christopher Myers (2000)

Easy Reading Books

Shoeshine Girl, Clyde Bulla (1975)
The Skirt, Gary Soto (1992)

Nonfiction

I Can't Accept Not Trying: Michael Jordan on the Pursuit of Excellence,
   Michael Jordan (1994)
Roberto Clemente, James Buckley, Jr. (2001)

Shooting for the Moon: The Amazing Life and Times of Annie Oakley, Stephen Krensky (2001)

Fiction

An Island Like You: Stories of the Barrio, Judith Ortiz Cofer (1995) (Pura Belpre Award)
Baseball in April and Other Short Stories, Gary Soto (1990)
Blackwater, Eve Bunting (1999)
Bluish, Virginia Hamilton (1999)
Brian's Return, Paulsen (1999)
Brian's Winter, Gary Paulsen (1996)
Esperanza Rising, Pam Muñoz Ryan (2000)
Hatchet, Gary Paulsen (1987)
Joey Pigza Loses Control, Jack Gantos (2000) (Newbery Honor)
Joey Pigza Swallowed the Key, Jack Gantos (1998)
Maniac Magee, Jerry Spinelli (1990) (Newbery Award)
Monster, Walter Dean Myers (1999) (National Book Award Finalist)
Scorpions, Walter Dean Myers (1988) (Newbery Honor)
Seedfolks, Paul Fleischman (1997)
Slam, Walter Dean Myers (1996) (Coretta Scott King Award)
Taking Sides, Gary Soto (1991)
The Laundry News, Andrew Clements (1999)
The Skin I'm In, Sharon G. Flake (1998) (Coretta Scott King Award)
What Do Fish Have to Do with Anything?, Avi (1997)
Wringer, Jerry Spinelli (1997) (Newbery Honor)

IMMIGRANTS

Picture Books

Going Home, Eve Bunting (1996)
Grandfather's Journey, Allen Say (1993) (Caldecott Medal)
I Have An Olive Tree, Eve Bunting (1999)

Easy Reading Books

Roberto Clemente, James Buckley, Jr. (2001)

Fiction

Baseball in April and Other Short Stories, Gary Soto (1990)
Esperanza Rising, Pam Muñoz Ryan (2000)
Seedfolks, Paul Fleischman (1997)

MYSTERY

Easy Reading Books

Aunt Eater Loves A Mystery, Dick King-Smith (1997)
Cam Jansen and the Catnapping Mystery, David Adler (1998)
Detective Dinosaur Lost and Found, James Skofield (1998)
Encyclopedia Brown and the Case of the Mysterious Handprints, Donald Sobol (1985)
Encyclopedia Brown and the Case of the Slippery Salamander, Donald Sobol (2000)
Ghost Town at Sundown, Mary Pope Osborne (1997)
In a Dark, Dark Room and Other Scary Stories, retold by Alvin Schwartz (1984)
Nate the Great and the Monster Mess, retold by Alvin Schwartz (1984)
Spider Kane and the Mystery at Jumbo Nightcrawler's, Mary Pope Osborne
The High-Rise Private Eyes: The Case of the Puzzling Possum, Cynthia Rylant (2001)
The Lucky Lottery, A to Z Mysteries, Ron Roy (2000)
The Missing Mummy, A to Z Mysteries, Ron Roy (2001)
The Panther Mystery: The Boxcar Children, created by Gertrude C. Warner (1998)

Fiction

Bunnicula: A Rabbit-Tale of Mystery, Deborah and James Howe (1979)
Bunnicula Strikes Again!, James Howe (1999)
Coffin on a Case, Eve Bunting (1992)
Dead Letter: A Herculeah Jones Mystery, Betsy Byars (1996)
Dew Drop Dead, James Howe (1990)
Holes, Lewis Sachar (1998) (Newbery Award)
Midnight Magic, Avi (1997)
The Lion Dance, Lawrence Yep (1998)
Who Stole the Wizard of Oz?, Avi (1981)

NONFICTION

Picture Books

A Blue Butterfly: A Story About Claude Monet, Bijou Le Tord (1995)
A Day in the Life of a Dancer, Linda Hayward (2001)
Diego, Jeanette and Jonah Winter (1991)
Franciso Goya, Mike Venezia (1991)
I Dreamed I Was a Ballerina, Anna Pavolva, illustrated by Edgar Degas (2001)
Leonardo's Horse, Jean Fritz (2001)
Martin's Big Words: The Life of Dr. Martin Luther King, Jr., Doreen Rappa-
    port (2001)
My Secret Camera: Life in the Lodz Ghetto, Frank Dabba Smith (2000)
Paul Gauguin, Mike Venezia (1993)
Red-Eyed Tree Frog, Joy Cowley (1999)
Shooting for the Moon: The Amazing Life and Times of Annie Oakley, Stephen
    Krensky (2001)
The Dinasours of Waterhouse Hawkins, Barbara Kerley (2001)

Easy Reading Books

Dinosaurs, Magic Tree House Research Guide, Will and Mary Pope Osborne
    (2000)
Free At Last! The Story of Martin Luther King, Jr., Angela Bull (2000)
Mummies and Pyramids, Magic Tree House Research Guide, Will and Mary
    Pope Osborne (2001)
NFL's Greatest Upsets, James Buckley, Jr. (2001)
Roberto Clemente, James Buckley, Jr. (2001)
Strikeout Kings, James Buckley, Jr. (2001)

Poetry

Insect Soup: Bug Poems, Barry Louis Polisar (1999)   ·

POETRY AND RHYMING VERSE

A Light in the Attic, Shel Silverstein (1981)
A Pizza the Size of the Sun, Jack Prelutsky (1994, 1996)
Brown Angels, Walter Dean Myers (1993)

Casey at the Bat: A Ballad of the Republic Sung in the Year 1888, Christopher Bing (2000) (Caldecott Honor)

Evertt Anderson's Goodbye, Lucille Clifton (1983) (Coretta Scott King Award)

Extra Innings: Baseball Poems, selected by Lee Bennett Hopkins (1993)

Falling Up, Shel Silverstein (1996)

For Laughing Out Loud: Poems to Tickle Your Funnybone, Jack Prelutsky (1991)

Green Eggs and Ham, Dr. Seuss (1960)

If Pigs Could Fly . . . And Other Deep Thoughts, Bruce Lansky (2000)

Insect Soup: Bug Poems, Barry Louis Polisar (1999)

No More Homework! No More Tests! Kids' Favorite Funny School Poems, selected by Bruce Lansky (1997)

Love That Dog, Sharon Creech (2001)

My Many Colored Days, Dr. Seuss (1996)

Oh, the Places You'll Go!, Dr. Seuss (1990)

Quiet Storm: Voices of Young Black Poets, selected by Lydia Omolola Okutoro (1999)

Salting the Ocean: 100 Poems by Young Poets, selected by Naomi Shihab Nye (2000)

Sports! Sports! Sports! A Poetry Collection, selected by Lee Bennett Hopkins (1999)

The Basket Counts, Arnold Adoff (2000)

The Cat in the Hat, Dr. Seuss (1957)

Where the Sidewalk Ends, Shel Silverstein (1974)

ROMANCE

Picture Books

Tea with Milk, Allen Say (1999)

Shooting for the Moon: The Amazing Life and Times of Annie Oakley, Stephen Krensky (2001)

Easy Reading Books

In Aunt Lucy's Kitchen—The Cobble Street Cousins, Cynthia Rylant (1998)

Sarah, Plain and Tall, Patricia MacLachlan (1985) (Newbery Medal)

Summer Party—The Cobble Street Cousins, Cynthia Rylant (2001)

The King's Equal, Katherine Patterson (1992)

Fiction

Beauty Lessons from An Island Like You: Stories of the Barrio, Judith Ortiz
   Cofer (1995) (Pura Belpre Award)
Broken Chain from Baseball in April and Other Stories, Gary Soto (1990)
Ella Enchanted, Gail Carson Levin (1997) (Newbery Honor)
Esperanza Rising, Pam Muñoz Ryan (2000)
Just Ella, Margaret Peterson Haddix (1999)

SPORTS

Picture Books

Hoops with Swoopes, Susan Kuklin with Sheryl Swoopes (2001)

Easy Reading Books

I Can't Accept Not Trying: Michael Jordan on the Pursuit of Excellence,
   Michael Jordan (1994)
NFL's Greatest Upsets, James Buckley, Jr. (2000)
Roberto Clemente, James Buckley, Jr. (2001)
Strikeout Kings, James Buckley, Jr. (2001)

Poetry

Casey at the Bat: A Ballad of the Republic Sung in the Year 1888, Christopher
   Bing (2000) (Caldecott Honor)
Extra Innings: Baseball Poems, selected by Lee Bennett Hopkins (1993)
Sports! Sports! Sports! A Poetry Collection, selected by Lee Bennett Hopkins
   (1999)
The Basket Counts, Arnold Adoff (2000)

Fiction

Baseball in April from Baseball in April and Other Stories, Gary Soto (1990)
Run, Billy, Run, Matt Christopher (1980)
Slam, Walter Dean Myers (1996)
Snowboard Maverick, Matt Christopher (1997)
Taking Sides, Gary Soto (1991)

Index

About the Author

Nancy S. Williams is a professor in the School of Education at DePaul University, Chicago, Illinois. She teaches courses in reading and children's literature, and supervises remediation practica in reading and learning disabilities. She received her Ph.D. from Northwestern University in the field of learning disabilities, her M.A. from Southern Methodist University as a reading specialist, and a B.A.E. from the University of Kansas in art education. She was an art instructor, reading specialist, learning disabilities resource room teacher, and a learning strategist in public elementary and secondary schools and has worked as a learning specialist and cognitive rehabilitation therapist in a hospital setting. She served as program coordinator in a collaborative university–school partnership program preparing career change individuals as teachers and served two years as associate dean in the School of Education. She has published articles about university–school partnerships, literacy, coauthored a book about developing literacy skills through trade books in clinical and classroom settings, and recently wrote a resource book for teachers about selecting and using quality children's literature with readability levels that are appropriate for struggling readers.